CHANGE
WE CAN
BELIEVE IN

Books by Barack Obama

Dreams from My Father:
A Story of Race and Inheritance

The Audacity of Hope:
Thoughts on Reclaiming the American Dream

CHANGE
WE CAN
BELIEVE IN

BARACK OBAMA'S PLAN
TO RENEW AMERICA'S PROMISE

With a Foreword by

BARACK OBAMA

CANONGATE
Edinburgh · London · New York · Melbourne

This paperback edition first published by
Canongate Books in 2009

I

First published in the United States in 2008 by Three Rivers
Press, an imprint of the Crown Publishing Group, a division of
Random House, Inc., New York
www.crownpublishing.com

First published in Great Britain in 2008 by Canongate Books Ltd,
14 High Street, Edinburgh EH1 1TE
www.meetatthegate.com

Grateful acknowledgment is made to the following: **Introduction**,
page 13: Tim Llewellyn; **Reviving Our Economy**, page 31: Polaris
Images/Scout Tufankjian; **Rebuilding America's Leadership**,
page 107: AP/Wide World Photos/Mikhail Metzel; **Conclusion**,
page 193: Michael Schneider; **The Call**, pages 200–201: David Katz

British Library Cataloguing-in-Publication Data
A catalogue record for this book is available on
request from the British Library

ISBN 978 1 84767 489 0

Design by Barbara Sturman

Printed and bound in Great Britain by Clays Ltd, St Ives plc

Obama for America's net proceeds will be donated to charity.

Contents

PART 2

THE CALL

CHANGE
WE CAN
BELIEVE IN

FOREWORD

EVERY so often, there are moments that define a generation.

For my grandfather, who marched in Patton's army, and my grandmother, who worked on a bomber assembly line while he was at war, it was the liberation of Europe and the rebuilding of an America that offered unrivaled opportunity and mobility for the middle class. Decades later, men and women from all walks of life marched and struggled and sacrificed for civil rights, women's rights, and worker's rights. Free people from across the world tore down a wall to end a cold war, while the revolutions in communications and technology that followed have reduced global barriers to prosperity and cooperation.

At the beginning of this young century, we face our own defining moment.

Our nation is in the middle of two wars—a war in Iraq

that must come to an end, and a war in Afghanistan that is and has always been the central front in the fight against terror. Our planet is in the midst of a climate crisis that, if we do not act, could devastate the world our children inherit. And our economy is in a downward spiral that is costing millions of Americans their homes, their jobs, and their faith in that fundamental promise of America—that no matter where you come from, or what you look like, or who your parents are, this is a country where you can make it if you try.

But in this moment of great challenge exists an even greater opportunity. For in my travels across this country, I have found that the disillusionment with Washington is not limited to any one party or group of people. It is shared by Democrats, independents, and even Republicans from all walks of life who are tired of being disappointed by the partisanship and petty politics that stop us from solving challenges like health care, energy, and education year after year. These Americans and millions more understand that at this moment in history, we just can't afford to keep doing what we've been doing. They are ready to come together and choose a new and better future for America.

This election offers that choice. And this book is about that future.

I have a vision for America rooted in the values that have always made our nation the last best hope of Earth—values that have been expressed to me on front porches and family farms; in church basements and town hall meetings over the last eighteen months. The people I've met know that government can't solve all our problems, and they don't expect it to. They believe in personal responsibility, hard work, and self-reliance. They don't like seeing their tax dollars wasted.

But they also believe in fairness, opportunity, and the responsibilities we have to one another. They believe in an America where good jobs are there for the willing, where hard work is rewarded with a decent living, and where we recognize the fundamental truth that Wall Street cannot prosper while Main Street crumbles—that a sound economy requires thriving businesses *and* flourishing families.

In a globalized world that has changed dramatically over the last few decades, forging this kind of future will not be easy. It will require new ways of thinking and a new spirit of cooperation. We'll need to work harder, and study more, and teach our children to replace the remote controls and video games with books and homework. And most of all, we'll need the kind of politics and policies in Washington that finally reflect the best values of America.

It won't be easy. It won't happen overnight. But I'm running for President because I believe that it's possible. I believe that if we seize this moment to look beyond our differences and focus on the challenges that affect us all, we can meet them. It's our choice.

We can choose to do nothing about disappearing jobs and shuttered factories for another four years, or we can decide that we'll have an economic policy that finally encourages growth and job creation in the United States of America. We can have a policy that ends the tax breaks for corporations that ship jobs overseas and gives them to companies that create jobs right here. We can create five million new green jobs that pay well and can't be outsourced by investing in renewable sources of energy like wind power, solar power, and the next generation biofuels. And we can create another two million jobs by investing in our crumbling infrastructure and building new schools, roads, and bridges. The choice is ours.

We can choose to let families who aren't sure if their next paycheck will cover next month's bills struggle on their own, or we can decide that if you work in this country, you will not want. We can give energy rebates to consumers who are having trouble filling up their gas tanks. We can give tax breaks to middle-class families and seniors instead of to Fortune 500 CEOs. We can lower health care premiums for those with insurance and make coverage affordable for those who don't have it. And we can provide working families with a nest egg and make it easier for them to save for retirement. We can choose that future.

We can allow ourselves to stay mired in the same education debate that has consumed Washington for decades, or we can come to a consensus that true progress on education will require both more resources and more reform. It will require investing in early-childhood education, recruiting an army of qualified teachers who we'll pay more and expect more from in return, and ensuring that a college education is affordable by offering free tuition in exchange for community or national service.

And most of all, it will require parents to get involved in their children's education early and often. I believe that if we truly want to help our children compete for the jobs of the future with children in Beijing and Bangalore, all of us have a role in ensuring that every child gets a world-class education from the day they're born to the day they graduate college.

We can continue to spend billions of dollars a month in Iraq and ask our overstretched military to stay there indefinitely, or we can rebuild that military, responsibly redeploy our brave men and women to finish the fight against Al Qaeda and the Taliban in Afghanistan, and renew our alliances to meet the threats of the twenty-first century.

These are the choices we face in November and over the next few years—decisions that will set the course for the next decade, if not the century. We can choose to remain on the failed path we've been traveling for so many years, or we can come together like so many generations before us and forge a future where we renew the promise at the very heart of the American idea—that this is a place where everyone has a chance to make it if you really try.

This is the promise that gave my grandfather the chance to go to college on the GI Bill after he returned from World War II, and allowed him and my grandmother to buy their first home with a loan from the Federal Housing Authority. It's the promise that led my father, who grew up herding goats in Kenya, to cross the ocean just for the chance to study in America. It allowed my mother, who raised my sister and me as a single parent without much money, to send us to some of the best schools in the country with the help of scholarships.

And it's the promise that first led me to Chicago all those years ago. After college, a lot of my friends went directly to law school or took jobs on Wall Street, and I initially did similar work. But when I stopped and thought about the chances I had been given—chances that so many others still didn't have—I decided that I would do my small part to change that. And so I took a job with a group of churches on the South Side that were trying to help neighborhoods that had been devastated by the closing of a steel plant.

We faced hard days and our share of failure, but I learned then that no matter how great the challenge or how difficult the circumstance, change is always possible if you're willing to work for it, and fight for it, and, above all, believe in it.

In the end, that is America's greatest gift to all those who choose to make a home on her endless frontier.

I have talked a great deal about change in this campaign, and the purpose of this book is to describe in detail what that change would look like. But as I have said many times in many places across this great nation, and as I learned all those years ago on the streets of Chicago, the only way to truly bring about the future we seek is if we're willing to work together as one nation, and one people. That is our task in the months and years ahead, and I look forward to joining all of you in that effort.

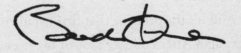

PART 1
THE PLAN

HOPE
FOR AMERICA

We stand at a moment of great challenge and great opportunity. All across America, a chorus of voices is swelling in a demand for change. The American people want the simple things that—for eight years—Washington hasn't delivered: an economy that honors the efforts of those who work hard, a national security policy that rallies the world to meet our shared threats and makes America safer, a politics that focuses on bringing people together across party lines to work for the common good. It's not too much to ask for. It is the change that the American people deserve.

Yet today our nation is at war, our economy is in turmoil, and our planet is in peril. American families are living with a health care system that costs more, delivers less, and bankrupts families and businesses; schools that fail to provide opportunity to too many of our children; and a retirement system that may not be able to pay out what it promised. Across the country, families are paying record prices to fill up their gas tanks and shopping carts. Too many Americans worry about whether they'll be able to raise their kids in safety and security and give them a shot at a better life.

But these challenges were not inevitable. They are the result of flawed policies and failed leadership. As our world and economy have changed, the thinking in Washington has not kept pace with the tests of the twenty-first century. Instead of investing in America's ability to compete or confronting the new national security challenges, we've seen tax cuts for the wealthiest Americans and an open-ended commitment to a war in Iraq that isn't making us safer and is distracting us from the real threats to our security. As a result, fewer Americans have reaped the benefits of the global economy, a growing number of Americans work harder for less, and our country is losing control over its destiny.

The first years of this new century should have been the moment when America's leaders had the strength to turn adversity into opportunity, the wisdom to see a little further down the road, and the courage to challenge conventional thinking and worn ideas. We could have reinvented our economy and responded to new threats in ways that seized the promise of the future.

Instead, these past eight years will be remembered for their rigid and ideological adherence to discredited ideas. Just think of what we *could* have done if we were united and worked together. Instead of making a real commitment to a world-class education for our kids and preparing them to seize the jobs of tomorrow, we passed "No Child Left Behind," a law that has the right goals but left the money behind and failed to empower teachers, principals, and school boards. Instead of ending our addiction to oil, we continued down a path that sends our dollars to dictators and tyrants, endangers our planet, and has left Americans struggling with $4-a-gallon gasoline. Instead of investing in innovation and rebuilding our crumbling roads and bridges, we spent billions in tax giveaways to the wealthiest of the wealthy. Instead of reducing soaring health care costs for all Americans, we did nothing and have seen premiums, co-pays, and out-of-pocket expenses spiral out of control. And instead of rallying the world to our side as we routed Al Qaeda, we spent hundreds of billions of dollars fighting a war in Iraq that should never have been authorized and never been waged.

The past eight years have been a failure of American leadership, not a failure of the American people.

Barack Obama believes that we can change course, and that we must. He looks to the future with optimism and hope. This is not the first time our nation has faced adversity, and each time we have, our people have summoned the will and found the way to conquer our challenges. This moment is no different. Working together, we can revive our economy and give every family the opportunity to succeed; we can lead the world to overcome the transnational security threats that imperil us; we can perfect our union by reinvigorating basic American values; and we can make investments now that will put America at the forefront of the new economy.

The choices in this election aren't between left and right, or Republican and Democrat. The choices we face are about the past versus the future.

To bring about real change, we need to start by creating a

new kind of politics that reconnects the American people with their government and offers not just a vote at the ballot box, but a voice in Washington that cannot be ignored. Americans from every background and every corner of our country yearn for a politics that brings us together instead of tears us apart. What they want—and what our nation needs—isn't blind, uncritical agreement. Americans don't agree on everything, nor should we. But behind all the labels and categories that define us, Americans are a decent, generous, and compassionate people, united by common challenges and common hopes. When that fundamental goodness and patriotism is called upon, our country responds. Barack Obama believes that deeply. As President, he will govern very differently than the current occupant of the Oval Office.

On his first day as President, Barack Obama will launch the most sweeping ethics reform in history to make the White House the people's house. Barack Obama will:

- Close the revolving door that has allowed government employees to use their administration jobs as a stepping-stone to further their lobbying careers.
- End the abuse of no-bid contracts and institute an absolute gift ban for political appointees.
- Hire people to serve not based on party or ideology, but only on qualification and experience.
- Use the Internet to make government more open and transparent so that anyone can see that Washington's business is the people's business.

As we fix Washington, we'll be able to respond to the great challenges our nation faces, and one of the biggest challenges is jump-starting our economy and ensuring that its opportunities are widely shared.

We know that America succeeds when the playing field is level and open, and people don't fall behind. Our economy is at its strongest when we reward work, not just wealth, and when all Americans can prosper from growth.

It is with our faith in these self-evident truths that we built the largest economy the world has ever known and the biggest middle class in history. But for the last eight years, we've failed to keep the fundamental promise that if you work hard you can live your own vision of the American Dream. Instead, our people are working harder for less, and we've lost more than 463,000 jobs in the first seven months of this year. The cost of everything from gas to groceries and college tuition is skyrocketing. Foreclosure activity is the highest it's been since the Great Depression, and housing values have fallen dramatically. Americans are finding it harder to save, retire, and juggle the demands of work and family. It's easy to feel as if that dream of boundless opportunity that should be the right of all Americans is slipping away.

These difficult times are not an accident of history. To be sure, some of these problems are a result of changes in our economy that no one can control. But the real struggle being waged in American homes and workplaces today is a consequence of tired and misguided economic policies in Washington. Instead of expanding opportunity for working people, Washington insiders heaped benefits on the wealthiest among us. Instead of making sure that people can live their dreams on Main Street, they tilted the scales for special interests and Wall Street. Instead of saying "We're all in this together," they pursued an economic policy that has one idea at its heart: "You're on your own."

Barack Obama believes that to steer us out of this downturn and to put America on course to lead in the global economy, we have to hold firm to one core principle: that our economy must grow to advance opportunity for all Americans. Because when it comes to our economy, the American people are not the problem; they are the answer. If more Americans are succeeding, our economy will be a success. This is a uniquely American idea, one that led us to build public high schools when we transitioned from a nation of farms to one of factories, sent the Greatest Generation to college on the GI Bill, and invested in science and research that have led to new discoveries and entire new industries.

To create widespread opportunity and economic prosperity in this new, global economy, we cannot simply look backward for solutions and hope that the New Deal and Great Society programs born of different eras are, by themselves, adequate to meet today's challenges. Nor can we try to fence off the world beyond our borders. Technology and globalization have triggered a fundamental change in the economy. There is no going back.

Instead, we must adapt our policies and our institutions to a new and changing world while holding fast to our bedrock principles. As President, Barack Obama will:

- Jump-start our economy with a $50 billion stimulus plan that will put money directly in the pockets of families struggling with rising food and mortgage payments.
- Restore simplicity, fairness, and values to the tax code

by rewarding work instead of wealth; giving 150 million middle-class workers and their families up to a $1,000 tax cut; totally eliminating income tax for seven million senior citizens; and making work pay by dramatically expanding the Earned Income Tax Credit.

- Sign into law a health care plan that guarantees affordable, quality insurance to every American who wants it; brings down premiums for every family who currently has coverage; boosts quality; requires coverage of preventative care; reduces the price of prescription drugs; and stops insurance companies from denying coverage based on preexisting conditions.

- Shore up Americans' retirements by creating automatic workplace retirement plans, strengthening Social Security, and protecting workers' pensions.

- Help workers share the benefits of economic growth by raising the minimum wage and giving workers a free choice about joining labor unions.

- Make college affordable for everyone willing to work for it through a new $4,000 American Opportunity Tax Credit and increasing the size of Pell Grants.

- Launch a new energy policy that will help ease the burden of high gasoline prices, free us from relying on monarchs and tyrants for our energy supplies, and slow global warming. The Obama plan will make significant investments in clean, renewable sources of energy, and create up to five million new green jobs.

- Keep America competitive by investing in our infrastructure—including roads, bridges, rails, locks and levees, and high-speed Internet—and by boosting our investments in scientific research that will be a key to America's success in the twenty-first century.

- Give every child a world-class education by recruiting an army of new teachers with better pay and more support; requiring higher standards and accountability from our classrooms; and telling the truth: that the best education starts with parents who turn off the TV, take away the video games, and are engaged in their children's lives.

Just as commerce, cargo, and capital pay little heed to the lines on a map in this globalized world, the same is true of the new challenges to our national security. For most of our history, national security threats arose from nation-states mustering armies and deploying navies in the pursuit of treasure or power. Even when the Soviet nuclear threat loomed large, our military, diplomatic, and economic strength, as well as the oceans that surround us, gave the United States a large degree of security. In fact, for the last century, not one of our battles was fought on the American mainland. In our new century, that has changed. New threats have emerged that know no boundaries, come from distant corners of the world, and increasingly pose a direct danger to America.

Weak and failing states from Africa to Central Asia to the Pacific Rim are incubators of resentment and anarchy that can become havens for terrorists and criminals. A global climate crisis is warming the planet with potentially devastating consequences. Killing fields in Rwanda, Congo, and Darfur have offended our humanity and set back the world's sense of collective security. A new age of nuclear proliferation and poorly secured nuclear material has left the world's deadliest weapons in the reach of an increasing number of countries from North Korea to Iran. And the very openness of our new world can be exploited for terror as we painfully learned on the morning of September 11. We will never forget the nearly three thousand Americans killed on 9/11— more than we lost at Pearl Harbor. And as we unite to combat this enemy, we must always remember that the attack did not come from a dictator, a country, or an empire. It came from stateless terrorists, who distort Islam and hate America, took refuge in Taliban-run Afghanistan, and masterminded a plot to kill innocent American men, women, and children with abandon.

After 9/11, our calling was to write a new chapter in the American story, turning tragedy into triumph. It's what we did in the Civil War as a conflict over states' rights became an opportunity to set the slaves free; after Pearl Harbor as that surprise attack led to a wave of freedom rolling across the Atlantic and Pacific; and during the Cold War as the lifting of the Iron Curtain galvanized us to build new institutions at home, establish strong international partnerships abroad, and stand firm for democratic values.

But our leaders in Washington never summoned us. They didn't seize the opportunity to devise new security strategies and build new alliances, to secure our homeland and safeguard our values, and to serve a just cause abroad. We were ready. Americans were united, and friends around the world stood shoulder to shoulder with us. We had on our side the might and moral force that is the legacy of generations of Americans. The tide of history seemed poised to turn, once again, toward hope.

But instead, we got a politics of fear that uses patriotism as a wedge to divide us. We got the diplomacy of "my way or the highway," where the United States—which had summit meetings with Soviet leaders at the height of the Cold War—refused to talk to our adversaries. We got a rigid twentieth-century theory of foreign affairs that insisted that the twenty-first century's stateless terrorism could be defeated through the invasion and occupation of a country— Iraq—that, while a horrible regime, had nothing to do with the attacks of 9/11.

Now, Osama bin Laden is still at large, and Al Qaeda has reconstituted itself in the tribal areas of Pakistan. We have neither developed the new capabilities needed to defeat a new enemy nor launched a comprehensive strategy to dry up the terrorists' base of support. We undermined our strength by compromising our values of due process and liberty and by not fully securing our homeland. And we went to war in Iraq—a war that Barack Obama opposed in 2002—with no plan for how to win the peace. This shifted our focus away from battling Al Qaeda, strained our military, divided our country, and diminished our global standing in the world.

In spite of all this, our men and women in uniform have performed bravely and brilliantly. They have done everything that has been asked of them—and much more—without nearly enough backup and support. They have been asked to bear an evolving and ever-increasing load: gathering intelligence, training foreign militaries, supplying earthquake and tsunami relief, fighting with Afghan allies to topple the Taliban, persevering in the deserts and cities of Iraq, and winning every battle they have fought. As it has in four different centuries, the U.S. military has answered when called, and the verdict on their performance is clear: through their commitment, their courage, and their capability, they have done us all proud.

But the sad truth is that they—and all of us—have not had civilian leadership that lives up to this service. It's time for new leadership in a changing world. In all he does as commander in chief, Barack Obama will be guided by the understanding that there is no more awesome responsibility that is placed in a President's hand than protecting our country and our security. As President, Barack Obama will:

- End the war in Iraq responsibly with a phased withdrawal that pushes Iraq's leaders toward a political solution, rebuilds our military, and refocuses our attention on defeating Osama bin Laden and Al Qaeda.
- Turn the tide against global terrorism with new military capabilities, enhanced intelligence, vigorous and tough diplomacy, a restoration of America's moral authority in the battle of ideas, and forward-looking, strengthened homeland security.
- Stop the spread of nuclear weapons through a comprehensive strategy for nuclear security that will reduce the danger of nuclear terrorism and prevent the spread of nuclear weapons capabilities.

- Rebuild a strong twenty-first-century military that has the training, equipment, and support it needs to respond to new threats.
- Rally the world against the new global threats of the twenty-first century—climate change, oil dependence, extreme poverty, disease pandemics, genocide, and failed states.
- Provide our members of the Armed Forces, wounded warriors, and veterans with the pay, care, benefits, and respect they and their families have earned.
- Lead the free world by rebuilding strong alliances and partnerships to more effectively confront the threats to our security, as well as tough, direct diplomacy even with our enemies. We must once again have the courage and conviction not to be afraid to let any dictator know where America stands and what we stand for.

As we confront these challenges, the conventional thinking in Washington tells us that we're a country divided into Red states and Blue states; that we're doomed to fight the same tired partisan battles over and over again; that we can't come together to grow our economy or meet the threats of the twenty-first century; that we can't take on big challenges like health care, energy, or education; that Americans can't reach past the lines of region, religion, or race; and that young Americans are unwilling to serve and act as citizens in the highest sense.

But at this moment, millions of Americans are already coming together to prove that thinking wrong and demand something better. They are hungry for new leadership and a new direction for America. These Americans are Democrats who are tired of being divided; Republicans who no longer recognize their own party; and independents who are ready for change in Washington. They are young people who've been inspired for the very first time and those not-so-young Americans who've been inspired for the first time in a long time. They include veterans and churchgoers, sportsmen and students, farmers and factory workers, and teachers and business owners. They all have varied backgrounds and different traditions, but they share the same values that bind us together as one country: common sense and honesty; generosity and compassion; decency and responsibility.

What we need in the next President is the proven ability to bring people to the table and get things done. We need a President who understands the world we live in today and has a detailed plan to bring opportunity and security to all Americans. We need a leader who will level with the American people about what he will do if entrusted with the presidency and what we, as a nation, must do to get our country back on track.

That is the kind of leader that Barack Obama has been his entire life. The pages ahead contain details about the substantive agenda that Barack Obama has put forward to the American people. We hope you read it, share it with your neighbors, and join the debate about what we should do at this critical time and what America can become. Taken together, these policies are more than just a compendium of what to expect from Barack Obama. They sum up his faith in what this country can be: that in the face of war, there can be security and peace; that in the face of despair, there can be hope; that in the face of a cynical partisanship that has divided us for too long, Americans can be one people united in building that more perfect union.

That's what this campaign—and this moment—are all about: change we can believe in.

REVIVING
OUR ECONOMY
STRENGTHENING THE MIDDLE CLASS

"I've often said that in the business world, the rear-view mirror is always clearer than the windshield. But I believe that Barack Obama has the right understanding of the fundamental challenges we face and the right vision for where we need to go as a nation. When my secretary pays taxes at a higher rate than I do, it's clear we need to restore that sense of fairness to our economy that allows all Americans a chance at the American Dream. Barack Obama will do that. His plan to strengthen the middle class will help all Americans move forward, which makes us all stronger—businesses and families alike."

—Warren Buffett

CEO and Chairman of Berkshire Hathaway, Inc.

"In eight years, real incomes have fallen, core expenses have risen, and millions of families, even those with two incomes, are working harder than ever just to make ends meet. Barack Obama boldly addresses issues critical to family economic security that other politicians avoid: predatory lending, rising bankruptcies, and staggering credit card debt. His policies will strengthen the middle class, restore the safety net, and help us live up to the ideal that here in America, we rise and fall together."

—Elizabeth Warren

Coauthor of *The Two-Income Trap: Why Middle-Class Mothers and Fathers Are Going Broke*

Throughout American history, our nation has grown and prospered when all Americans have shared in the opportunities created by our economy. Despite all the changes in our world, Barack Obama believes that this is still the road to prosperity today. He believes that we must create bottom-up growth that empowers hardworking families to climb the ladder of success and raise their children with security, opportunity, and hope for a better future. These hopes are at the heart of the American Dream. Yet, despite the resilience, optimism, and hard work of the American people, their dreams too often have been frustrated over the last eight years by economic policies that protect special interests and the privileged few and ignore the working families that are America's backbone and the engine of our economic growth.

No one reading this book needs to be told that our economy is hurting. The price of filling up the gas tank or filling up a shopping cart has skyrocketed over the past several months. American families are working harder and making less. Jobs are disappearing—463,000 in the first seven months of this year, and over three million manufacturing jobs have been lost since George W. Bush took office. Foreclosures have hit their highest level since the Great Depression, and housing values have fallen dramatically. Nest eggs are cracking as the stock market struggles. The costs of health care and college tuition have gone through the roof. Too many families are one major incident—a sudden illness, a pink slip, or a car accident—away from falling off the ladder of economic opportunity and out of the middle class.

Just as the revolutions in technology and communications have opened new avenues of opportunity for American workers and businesses, they also have made it possible for companies to send jobs wherever there is an Internet connection. Countries like India and China that once were laggards have leapt ahead to provide goods and services to companies and consumers all over the world. Our workers and our businesses in almost every sector are now facing competition from all over the globe.

Fortunately, Americans are the most creative, industrious people in the world. Our inventions have changed people's lives across the globe. Our hard work has built whole new industries and given generations the promise of lives better than those their parents had. Our companies and our workers can outthink and outperform anyone anywhere if we set fair rules and let them succeed.

Yet in the face of rising competition, Washington has stood still—and in some cases, even moved backward. In the last eight years, the Administration has abandoned the principle of broad-based growth that has been the historic foundation of our success. Instead this Administration has fully embraced the discredited philosophy of trickle-down economics that believes that big tax breaks for the wealthiest will eventually work their way to all. They have given massive tax breaks to big corporations and billionaires while allowing high-priced lobbyists to rig the game for their well-heeled clients.

As we have seen, that approach has failed. The sad truth is that we did not arrive at the current economic emergency by some accident of history. This was not an inevitable part of the business cycle that was beyond our power to avoid. It was the unavoidable conclusion of a tired and misguided philosophy that has dominated Washington for far too long.

By sacrificing critical investments in health care, education, energy, and technology to pay for trillions of dollars in tax breaks for the wealthy and well-connected; by abandoning all pretense of fiscal responsibility and forcing our country to borrow its money from foreign countries like China and Saudi Arabia while leaving our children to foot the bill; by ignoring the squeeze on ordinary Americans and making it harder for them to get ahead, this Administration has walked away from the broad-based growth that has made this country great.

Barack Obama has a very different vision—one that will move our economy forward and keep us at the cutting edge in the global economy. He will put the needs of working- and middle-class Americans first, rather than those of special interests and corporate lobbyists. He has a real plan to get the economy moving again, create jobs, and drive up wages and incomes. Barack Obama knows that our economy is strongest when all Americans prosper; when the middle class is growing and succeeds, all of us succeed. He believes that we must move decisively to revive our sputtering economy. At the same time, we must invest in America's future prosperity—with a bold, new energy strategy; revamped schools; affordable, high-quality health care; and a twenty-first-century infrastructure.

Barack Obama's emergency economic plan to immediately jump-start our economy will give a $1,000 rebate that middle-class families could use to pay for the soaring price of gasoline, the rising price of food, or help with other necessities.

Barack Obama also has a plan to expand opportunity and ensure growth over the long run through smart investments in America and Americans. To make sure our kids and our country can compete globally, Barack Obama believes our schools must meet higher standards. He has a plan to require greater accountability to create world-class schools and to recruit a generation of new teachers. As President, Barack Obama will help employers by bringing down the cost of health care, so they can invest and grow. And an Obama Administration will invest $150 billion over ten years in renewable energy industries, creating millions of new jobs.

With our economy struggling, Barack Obama's plan makes the investments we need to grow our economy so that every American has a chance to succeed.

Provide Immediate Relief with an Emergency Economic Plan

We are facing one of the worst economic crises in a generation, in part because of policy choices made by this Administration. With families struggling, Barack Obama recognizes that we cannot wait until January 2009 to change our economic course. We can neither stand by idly as millions of families are struggling and our future prosperity is at risk nor assume that more of the same tax cuts for corporations and the wealthy will get us out of this problem. That is why Barack Obama believes that we need an emergency economic plan to jump-start the economy, help families offset some of the costs of filling up the gas tank and surging food prices, prevent the layoff of one million workers, and get our economy back on track. His emergency economic plan will:

Send Rebate Checks of $1,000 to American Families.

It's just wrong that while millions of American families are struggling to pay their utility bills, fill up their gas tanks, and cover escalating day-to-day costs, big oil companies are posting record profits. Under the Obama stimulus plan, a portion of big oil companies' windfall profits will be used to fund direct relief worth $500 for an individual and $1,000 for a married couple. The relief would be delivered as quickly as possible, and would be a down payment on the middle-class tax cut Barack Obama will implement as President. This sizable relief would be fully paid for with five years of a windfall profits tax on record oil company profits.

Save One Million Jobs.

Rebuilding our crumbling roads and bridges and renovating our schools is not just smart long-term economic policy; it also will provide a short-term boost to our economy. Barack Obama believes that we should establish a $25 billion Jobs and Growth Fund to replenish the Highway Trust Fund; prevent cutbacks in road and bridge maintenance; and fund new, fast-tracked projects to repair schools. Taken together, this would save one million jobs that would be in danger of disappearing if this funding was not available.

Help Local Communities Through Tough Times.

Because of the housing crisis and the weakening economy, property values are plummeting, and many state and local governments are suddenly facing significant revenue shortfalls. Barack Obama believes that in the areas hardest hit by the housing crisis, we should provide immediate, temporary funding of $25 billion to state and local governments. This

> "Instead of handing out giveaways to corporations that don't need them and didn't ask for them, it's time we started giving a hand up to families who are trying to pay their medical bills and send their children to college."
>
> —BARACK OBAMA, June 9, 2008, Raleigh, North Carolina

money would help ensure that vital services—such as police, fire, education, and health care—are not the victims of this downturn. States and localities also could use a portion of the money to pursue innovative approaches to reducing the impact that foreclosures have on communities. In addition, this initiative will ensure that there is sufficient funding to help hard-pressed families afford home heating and weatherization as we move into the fall and winter months.

Economic Security and Opportunity for All American Families

Throughout every transformation the American economy has made—from agriculture to industry, local to national, peace to war and back again—there has been one constant: the advancement of individual opportunity. This isn't a guarantee of success. But, as Americans, we believe that if you work hard, your work will be rewarded—that everyone should have an equal shot of making a good living, raising a family, giving their children a good start in life, and enjoying a secure retirement.

Right now, instead of a tax code that helps create opportunity for all, we have a tax code that is open to the highest bidder, riddled with loopholes, and gamed to help the wealthy and well-connected. This is the same dynamic that has thwarted progress on reducing the costs of health care and college and making sure that all our children go to schools that prepare them for success. As a result, the promise of upward mobility is more and more difficult for hard-working families to realize.

At the same time, higher health care, energy, and college costs together with falling incomes have made it harder for families to save and have the resources to go back to school, start a new business, or plan for their future. This economic insecurity makes it harder for families to invest in their future, which ultimately means less growth and less investment in all of our future. It chokes off the dynamism and risk-taking that make America the most innovative economy in the world. Barack Obama's plan throws out what doesn't work, like tax breaks for big oil companies and companies that ship jobs overseas, and invests in what does work, such as tax breaks for businesses that create American jobs and support for hardworking families. As President, Barack Obama will:

Give Every Working Family a $1,000 Tax Cut.

To give 150 million workers the tax relief they deserve, Barack Obama will create a new "Making Work Pay" tax credit of up to $500 per person, or $1,000 per working family. This refundable income tax credit will offset the payroll tax on the first $8,100 of earnings for 95 percent of all American workers while still preserving the important principle of a dedicated revenue source for Social Security. This not only helps small business owners struggling to meet expenses; for 10 million low-income Americans, the "Making Work Pay" tax credit also will completely eliminate their federal income taxes. This tax cut is just part of a series of tax cuts that Barack Obama will give to help American families afford a new home, pay for college and health care, and save for retirement. For tens of millions of families, Barack Obama's tax cuts will provide thousands of dollars of needed relief.

Eliminate Income Taxes for Seniors Making Less than $50,000.

Barack Obama believes that seniors facing high health care costs and who are worrying about dwindling retirement savings also need relief. As President, he will eliminate all income taxes for seniors making less than $50,000 per year. This will save seven million seniors an average of $1,400 a year, and mean that twenty-seven million seniors will not need to file an income tax return at all.

Ease the Burden of High Gas Prices and Make Oil Companies Share in the Sacrifice.

The most important step we can take to directly relieve the burden of rising gas prices is to give energy rebates that go directly into the pockets of families and provide relief at the pump, including a limited swap of oil from the Strategic Petroleum Reserve. We also should do everything we can to make sure that oil prices are not being driven up by speculators and that oil companies are not profiting unfairly from the windfall. That is why as President, Barack Obama would crack down on speculators by fully closing the "Enron loophole," a move that would require that U.S. energy futures trade on regulated exchanges. In addition, he will direct the Federal Trade Commission (FTC) and Department of Justice to investigate allegations of market manipulation and other wrongdoing.

Help Workers Displaced by Trade and Globalization.

To help all workers adapt to a rapidly changing economy, Barack Obama will modernize and expand the existing system of Trade Adjustment Assistance (TAA) to include all workers hurt by changing trade patterns—including those in the service sector and those losing jobs going to countries with which we do not have trade agreements, such as China and India. He will create flexible education accounts that workers can use to retrain, provide retraining assistance for workers in sectors of the economy vulnerable to dislocation before they lose their jobs, and provide additional assistance for workers to afford health care. He will also sign into law an updated WARN Act that requires large employers to notify employees of a layoff ninety days before a plant closing—an increase of thirty days from today's standard. And Barack Obama will expand apprenticeship programs to help workers get credentials and skills in crafts that reward that investment with a middle-class income and benefits.

Expand the Earned Income Tax Credit.

Those who work hard, full-time, should be able to make ends meet, yet too many working Americans cannot. In the Illinois State Senate, Barack Obama led the successful effort to create the $100 million Illinois Earned Income Tax Credit (EITC). As President, Barack Obama will reward work by increasing the number of working parents eligible for EITC benefits, the benefit available to parents who support their children through child support payments, and the benefit for families with three or more children—while reducing the EITC marriage penalty, which hurts low-income families. In an Obama Administration, full-time workers earning the minimum wage could see their EITC benefit triple.

Raise the Minimum Wage.

Barack Obama believes that people who work full-time should not live in poverty. Before the Democrats took back Congress, the minimum wage had not changed in ten years. Even though the minimum wage will rise to $7.25 an hour by 2009, the minimum wage's real purchasing power will still be below what it was in 1968. As President, Barack Obama will raise the minimum wage to $9.50 an hour by 2011 and index it to inflation.

Protect Workers and Their Right to Organize.

Barack Obama has seen firsthand how important unions are to ensuring fairness and dignity for workers. As a community organizer in a South Chicago neighborhood devastated by steel mill closings, Barack Obama saw what an important force for progress unions are. That's why he has championed organized labor for his entire career, and as President, Barack Obama will:

- Support and sign into law the Employee Free Choice Act to ensure that workers can exercise their right to organize, and oppose "Right-to-Work" and "Paycheck Protection" efforts to limit union membership and labor's voice.
- Ensure that workers are paid the wages and benefits

they have earned by upholding overtime pay protections and ensuring employers do not misclassify workers as "independent contractors" to avoid giving workers the benefits they deserve.

- Protect the Davis-Bacon Act on prevailing wages.
- Ban the permanent replacement of striking workers, so workers can stand up for themselves without worrying about losing their livelihoods.
- Make workplaces safer by increasing funding for the Occupational Safety and Health Administration, hire more inspectors, and increase penalties for lawbreakers.

Establish a Credit Card Bill of Rights.

As strapped consumers face mounting bills and declining home values, credit cards could turn into the next subprime market crisis. Barack Obama believes that every American should have a uniform set of rights while dealing with credit card companies, no matter their financial status or credit history. An Obama Administration will create a Credit Card Bill of Rights to ban unilateral changes, apply interest rate increases only to future debt, prohibit interest on fees, prohibit universal defaults, and require prompt and fair crediting of cardholder payments. It also will establish a five-star rating system, enforced by the FTC, to let consumers know about the level of risk involved in every credit card. Finally, credit card companies will be required to disclose in simplified, clear language all of the major features of the card along with their FTC rating so that consumers will have the information they need to compare credit card products.

Cap Exorbitant Interest Rates and Improve Disclosure.

In the wake of reports that some members of the military were paying 800 percent interest on payday loans, Congress took bipartisan action to limit interest rates charged to service members to 36 percent. Barack Obama believes that we must extend this protection to all Americans, because predatory lending continues to be a major problem for low- and middle-income families alike. He also believes that we need to ensure that all Americans have access to clear and simplified information about loan fees, payments, and penalties, which is why he'll require lenders to provide this information during the loan application process. An Obama Administration also will work to empower more Americans in the fight against predatory lending by supporting initiatives to improve financial literacy and financial planning and by encouraging banks and other financial institutions to provide short-term, small-dollar loans.

Restore Fairness to Bankruptcy Rules.

Barack Obama opposed the 2005 bankruptcy law, which favored banks over working families. As President, Barack Obama will restore fairness to our bankruptcy laws by providing an exemption for people who can prove they filed for bankruptcy because of medical expenses and expanding protections for military families and victims of natural disasters. He also will close the loophole in bankruptcy law that prevents families from renegotiating their mortgages so they can keep their homes.

Give Family Farmers the Stability They Need to Thrive.

Barack Obama believes that our farm programs and supports should go to help family farmers—not large agricultural companies—survive and thrive. As President, he will fight for farm programs that are targeted directly at family farmers, giving them the stability and predictability they need to succeed. An Obama Administration will support an effective payment limitation of $250,000 so taxpayers aren't underwriting big agribusinesses. Most important, it will close the loopholes that allow mega-farms to get around the limits by subdividing their operations into multiple paper corporations. Finally, an Obama Administration will make agriculture disaster assistance permanent.

Affordable Health Care for All Americans

One of the biggest drains on Americans' pocketbooks is the high cost of health care, and among the biggest insecurities that families face are the threat of losing their health care coverage or getting sick or injured and not being able to afford high-quality care. Health care premiums have nearly doubled in the past six years—while wages have stayed flat. In 2006, 11 million insured Americans spent more than a quarter of their salary on health care. The number of uninsured in America has jumped by 8.6 million under the current Administration, and now totals 47 million Americans. Many of those are people who insurers will not cover because they have existing medical problems. Millions more have insurance, but could be dropped as soon as they develop a serious medical problem. These Americans not only suffer, but they place a growing burden on the rest of us: every time an uninsured person walks into an emergency room because they have nowhere else to turn, there is a hidden tax on the rest of us as premiums go up—by an extra $922 per family in 2005 alone.

At the same time, businesses are finding it difficult to compete because of the high cost of premiums and the high cost of workers without access to high-quality care. Costs have gotten so high that more than half of all small companies can no longer afford to insure their workers, and some of the nation's biggest employers are being severely disadvantaged in the global marketplace by the high cost of care.

To make matters worse, a large amount of the money we spend is lost to massive waste and inefficiency. One out of every four dollars is swallowed up by administrative costs. Each year, 100,000 Americans die due to medical errors, and we lose $100 billion because of prescription drug errors alone. Only four cents of every dollar spent on health care goes to preventive care. And while the United States leads the world in health care expenditures, twenty-nine other countries have a higher life expectancy, and thirty-eight other nations have lower infant mortality rates.

For years, candidates have made promises about fixing health care and cutting costs, but when they go to Washington nothing happens because big drug and insurance companies use their deep pockets and clout to block reform. In the last five years, the fastest growing part of health costs has been what the insurance companies have kept to cover their costs and fatten their profits; the second fastest has been what the big drug companies charge for their medicines. Barack Obama has taken on the special interests in the past and expanded health coverage and improved quality. As President, he will take them on again to pass a health care plan that will cover every American and bring down the cost for high-quality care. The Obama plan will:

Lower Costs by $2,500 per Family and Improve Quality.

Health care spending is expected to double within the next decade even though Americans already spend almost twice as much per person as citizens of other industrialized countries and receive poorer health outcomes. Under the Obama plan, the typical family will have lower costs of $2,500 each year. To lower these costs and improve quality, Barack Obama will:

- Make an up-front investment of $50 billion in electronic health information technology systems to reduce errors, and save lives and money.
- Reduce the costs of catastrophic illnesses for employers and their employees by reimbursing employers for a portion of costs if savings were used to lower workers' premiums.
- Require disease management programs and integrated preventive care to help bring down the costs of caring for people with chronic conditions such as diabetes, heart disease, and high blood pressure.
- Require health plans to disclose what percentage of premiums actually goes to patient care as opposed to administrative costs.

> *"I want to wake up and know that every single American has health care when they need it, that every senior has prescription drugs they can afford, and that no parents are going to bed at night worrying about how they'll afford medicine for a sick child. That's the future we can build together."*
>
> —BARACK OBAMA, June 5, 2008, Bristol, Virginia

- Launch a comprehensive effort to tackle health care disparities.
- Reform medical malpractice while preserving patient rights, and strengthen antitrust laws to prevent insurers from overcharging doctors for malpractice insurance.
- Eliminate the excessive subsidies paid to Medicare Advantage plans and pay them the same amount it would cost to treat the same patients under traditional Medicare.

Guarantee Health Coverage for Every American.

Barack Obama's health care plan both builds on and improves the current insurance system, and leaves Medicare intact for seniors. For all Americans who like their health insurance, nothing changes except that they will have lower costs—$2,500 for a typical family. For those who do not have health insurance or who do not like their health insurance, they will have a range of private insurance options—accessible through a new National Health Insurance Exchange that is similar to what members of Congress have—as well as a public plan. The public plan will cover all essential medical services—including preventive, maternity, disease management, and mental health care. Costs will be low, but Americans who cannot afford it and do not qualify for Medicaid or SCHIP will receive a tax subsidy to pay for coverage. The health insurance coverage will be portable among jobs, easy to enroll in and use, and of high quality. Finally, to provide an incentive for small businesses to provide health insurance, Barack Obama will provide a refundable tax credit worth up to 50 percent on premiums paid to these companies.

Bring Down the Costs of Prescription Drugs.

The second-fastest growing type of health expense is the cost of prescription drugs. Americans should be able to afford the cutting-edge cures that our pharmaceutical industry develops. To bring down the costs of prescription drugs, an Obama Administration will:

- Allow Americans to import inexpensive and safe prescription drugs from countries where the same medicines are cheaper.
- Increase the use of generic drugs in all public health plans, stop large drug companies from paying to keep generics out of markets to preserve their profits, and create a pathway to bring generic vaccines and other biologic medicines to the market.
- Allow Medicare to negotiate for better prices.

Promote Prevention.

In the absence of a dramatic shift toward preventing illness and promoting public health, we will not be successful in containing medical costs or improving the health of the American people. Obesity is an epidemic that is seriously impacting the health of millions of Americans—especially children—and one-third of all Americans are living with a chronic condition. If we put more of our health care funds into prevention, we could save tens of millions of dollars and improve millions of people's lives. As President, Barack Obama will work with every sector of society—employers, school systems, community groups, and families—to ensure that Americans have access to preventive care. He will require that all federally supported health care plans cover these services, and will support efforts to promote healthy habits, lifestyles, and environments.

Empower Families to Succeed

It's not enough to just get families back on their feet. To get our economic engine humming again and to grow the middle class, we need to expand opportunity for all Americans. We need to make it easier for families to get an education, put away a nest egg, own a home, start a business, and provide a better life for their children. And we need to discard the outdated policies that don't work and invest in what works—what actually expands opportunity and enables America to compete globally. To empower American families to succeed, Barack Obama will:

Ensure That Every Child Gets a World-Class Education.

Now more than ever, success in the world economy begins at the schoolhouse door. A good education is critical for being able to live one's dreams. Moreover, attracting and growing good jobs here at home relies on having a highly educated, skilled workforce. That's why we must start investing in our people as soon as we can by giving every child a world-class education—in science, math, English, history, civics, and the arts. As President, Barack Obama will make a historic commitment to our children's education. He will set high standards and improve accountability—and give our schools the resources they need to meet those standards. He will recruit, prepare, retain, and reward a generation of new teachers. An Obama Administration will encourage additional learning time in schools and double funding for after-school programs to serve one million more kids. And Barack Obama will invest in zero-to-five early childhood education so that more children will have the best start they can at learning and life.

Make College Affordable for Everyone.

The cost of going to college has grown nearly 40 percent in the past five years. If we do not act now, by 2010, it's estimated that over the previous ten years, two million academically qualified students will not go to college because they can't afford it. Opening the doors of colleges to all who want to enter them is an investment in America worth making. As President, Barack Obama will create a new $4,000 American Opportunity Tax Credit to make community college completely free and cover two-thirds of the cost of tuition at the typical public university. Recipients of this credit will be required to conduct 100 hours of public service a year. He will simplify and streamline the financial aid application process, increase the maximum limit for Pell Grants, and eliminate federal subsidies to private student loan companies.

Create Automatic Workplace Pensions.

Currently, seventy-five million working Americans—roughly half the workforce—lack employer-based retirement plans. Even when workers are given the option of joining employer-based plans, many do not take up the option because it requires considerable work to research plans and investment portfolios as well as enroll. Barack Obama wants to change that by automatically enrolling workers in a workplace pension plan. Under his proposal, employers who do not currently offer a retirement plan will be required to enroll their employees in a direct-deposit IRA account that is compatible to existing direct-deposit payroll systems, and any employee is allowed to opt out if they do not want to participate. Under the Obama plan, when employees change jobs, their savings will be automatically rolled over into the new employer's system to ensure continued savings. Experts estimate that this program will more than quadruple the savings participation rate for low- and middle-income workers to as much as 80 percent. Over a lifetime, a typical worker using the Obama plan could add hundreds of thousands of dollars to his or her retirement savings.

Expand the Savers' Tax Credit for Working Families.

As President, Barack Obama will help working families save for retirement by expanding the existing Savers' Tax Credit to match 50 percent of the first $1,000 of savings for families that earn under $75,000, and he will make the tax credit refundable. The savings match will be automatically deposited into designated personal accounts by using the account information listed on IRS tax filings.

Preserve Social Security.

Barack Obama believes that Social Security is indispensable to workers and seniors, and he is committed to ensuring Social Security is solvent and viable for the American people, now and in the future. Although the underlying Social Security system remains strong, the program faces a challenge driven by our changing demographics. Barack Obama believes that we owe it to working families and retirees to guarantee Social Security for generations to come without undermining what makes it the most important public program in the first place: a solid, guaranteed bedrock of retirement security for hardworking families. He does not believe we need to raise the retirement age; will oppose any attempt to privatize Social Security, which would reduce benefits and explode the national debt; and believes it is critical that middle-class families are protected from tax increases or benefit cuts. Instead, Barack Obama would work with members of both parties to ensure that people making over $250,000 would pay a little more to help strengthen this program.

Protect Workers' Pensions.

Barack Obama believes we must ensure that private companies properly fund their pension plans so workers have the retirement security they earned and taxpayers do not end up footing the bill. Workers deserve to know where their money is going; this information also serves as a check on imprudent or fraudulent investments by fund managers. As President, Barack Obama will ensure that all employees who have company pensions receive annual disclosures about their pension fund's investments, including full details about where their savings have been invested, the performance of those investments, and appropriate details about probable future investments strategies. He also will reform corporate bankruptcy laws so that workers' retirements are one of the most important priorities for funding and workers aren't left with a bunch of worthless IOU's after years of service.

Secure Homeownership for American Families.

Owning one's home is an integral part of the American Dream. Barack Obama was an early sponsor of the housing legislation recently signed into law that will help prevent hundreds of thousands of home foreclosures, provide critical support to communities that have been hard hit by the housing crisis, and create a badly needed affordable housing trust fund. But we need to do more, including taking long-term steps to prevent these problems from reoccurring. To this end, Barack Obama will:

- Provide ten million middle-class homeowners 10 percent off their interest rate through a universal mortgage tax credit.
- Close the mortgage company loophole that prevents families from renegotiating mortgages in bankruptcy court.

- Crack down on unscrupulous mortgage-lending practices and help prevent future housing crises by passing the STOP FRAUD Act.
- Create a Homeowner Obligation Made Explicit (HOME) score, which will provide potential borrowers with a simplified, standardized borrower metric (similar to APR) for home mortgages.

Make It Easier to Balance Work and Family.

Americans are finding it harder and harder to juggle the demands of work and of family. Not only are many parents struggling to find safe, enriching child care, but many are also now finding themselves caring for their aging and infirm parents. Meanwhile, too many of our workplaces are not set up to reflect the new realities of working parents with many familial demands. As a father of two young children and husband of a working woman, Barack Obama understands these demands deeply. As President, he will help families with their daily juggle to balance work and family. Specifically, an Obama Administration will:

- Expand the Family and Medical Leave Act to cover more employees, to allow workers to take leave for elder care needs and for up to twenty-four hours each year to participate in their children's academic activities, and to address domestic violence issues.
- Provide funding to help all fifty states adopt paid family and medical leave.
- Require employers to provide seven paid sick days per year.

> *"For decades we've had politicians in Washington who talk about family values, but we haven't had policies that value families . . . that's why Washington has to change."*
>
> —BARACK OBAMA, June 23, 2008, Albuquerque, New Mexico

- Increase high-quality after-school and summer learning opportunities to two million additional children.
- Promote flexible work arrangements, such as telecommuting and nontraditional work schedules.
- Improve the Child and Dependent Care Tax Credit by making it refundable and allowing low-income families to receive up to a 50 percent credit for their child care expenses. This proposal will benefit an additional 7.5 million working women.
- Protect against caregiver discrimination by enforcing the recently enacted Equal Employment Opportunity Commission guidelines on caregiver discrimination.
- Fight for pay equity and close the gap between what women and men make for doing the same work.

Bring Opportunity to Areas of Concentrated Poverty.

Alleviating concentrated, intergenerational poverty is a difficult task, but there are comprehensive approaches that are successful in addressing the full range of obstacles that stand in the way of poor children. As President, Barack Obama will create twenty "Promise Neighborhoods" in cities that have high levels of poverty and crime and low levels of student academic achievement. The Promise Neighborhoods will follow the model of the highly successful Harlem Children's Zone and seek to engage children and their parents into an achievement program based on tangible goals, including college for every participating student and strong physical and mental health outcomes for children, as well as retention of meaningful employment and parenting schools for parents.

Restore Trust, Return to Fiscal Responsibility

Every family in America has to reconcile what they spend with what they have; they must find a way to pay the mortgage, monthly bills, and insurance premiums; put food on the table and fill up the gas tank; and sock whatever they can away for a rainy day or to send a son or daughter to college—all at the same time. Often, it's a struggle. But at the end of the year, the family budget has to add up. It's the same for our entrepreneurs and for our largest corporations.

But over the past eight years, Washington has ignored those rules and we have seen a dangerous erosion of the principles that have allowed our economy to thrive. Those who can make big campaign contributions or hire high-priced lobbyists are able to carve out huge loopholes in our tax code and win massive subsidies that shift the tax burden to small businesses and the middle class. Massive tax cuts have gone to the wealthiest individuals and hundreds of bil-

lions of dollars on tax breaks have been showered on big corporations. More than a half-trillion dollars have been spent
on invading and occupying Iraq. Large future expenditures
have routinely been omitted from the budget to mask their
true cost. In total, legislation enacted over the last eight
years has added $4 trillion to the deficit. As a result, we have
seen a surplus of $236 billion at the end of the Clinton Ad-
ministration that was projected to grow still larger over time
instead turn into a deficit of more than $400 billion today.
This has been the most fiscally irresponsible Administration
in American history.

Barack Obama will change how the government spends
your money. He will restore honest, transparent government. He will make sure Washington spends taxpayer dollars wisely—investing in the future, not mortgaging it. He
will modernize and simplify our tax code so that it provides
greater relief to more Americans. He will lead an Administration that will make sure its numbers add up, and the result
will be economic growth and prosperity for all Americans.
As President, Barack Obama will:

Pay for All Proposals and Cut the Deficit.

Barack Obama recognizes that when you are in a deep fiscal
hole, the first thing you do is stop digging. That is why he will
pay for all of his proposals and reduce the deficit. We cannot
afford another four years of a President who uses balanced
budget targets as a political sound bite while actually adding
hundreds of billions of dollars to our national debt. With
the current uncertainty surrounding the state of our economy, Barack Obama believes the best way to demonstrate a

genuine commitment to fiscal responsibility is to lay out how he will pay for all new proposals, return to conservative budget practices, and put forward tangible plans for immediate deficit reduction.

Cut Spending and Reduce Government Waste.

Barack Obama's budget plan is a net spending cut—all of his new investments are more than paid for by cutting wasteful spending and streamlining government. As President, Barack Obama will cut spending by responsibly ending the war in Iraq, cutting subsidies for private plans in Medicare, eliminating subsidies for private student loan companies, reforming agricultural subsidies for high-income farmers, continuing the progress Democrats have made on earmarks by cutting them to at least the level they were in 1994, ending no-bid contracting, and phasing out unnecessary and duplicative programs. In an Obama Administration, overall spending will be lower than the average level of the last forty years, as well as lower than the average level under the current President.

Put Medicare on Solid Footing by Reducing Costs and Improving Quality.

Barack Obama understands that the biggest threat to our fiscal future is the fact that health costs system-wide, in both the public and private sectors, are growing rapidly. While some want to deal with this long-term fiscal threat by simply cutting benefits for Medicare and Medicaid and turning them into a second-class health system, Barack Obama believes that will violate the trust we have made with our nation's seniors. As President, Barack Obama will put Medicare on sound fiscal footing by reducing health costs throughout our health system while improving quality.

Give Tax Relief to the 98 Percent of Households Making Less than $250,000 a Year.

The Bush tax cuts dangerously distorted our tax system by rewarding pure wealth and not rewarding hard work and success. Over the past eight years, the wealthiest of the wealthy have enjoyed large income gains while almost every single other American has struggled. Barack Obama believes that the rest of America deserves a break. As President, he will vow to not increase taxes for any household making less than $250,000 a year. That means that 98 percent of all households—and nearly 99 percent of small business owners—will not see their taxes rise. At the same time, the Obama plan will ask families making over $250,000 a year to give up a portion of the tax cuts they have gotten in recent years in order to restore fairness to our system without increasing the deficit.

Eliminate Special Tax Breaks for Corporations.

According to a recent congressional investigation, offshore tax abuse costs this country up to $100 billion each year. Almost half of all foreign profits of U.S. corporations in a recent year were hidden in tax havens, and as many as two million individual taxpayers may be hiding funds in offshore tax havens as well. Barack Obama has been a leader in cracking down on tax havens by requiring greater disclosure of financial transactions in tax secrecy jurisdictions and giving the Treasury Department the tools and time it needs to enforce the law. In addition, the tax code is filled with special provisions that subsidize companies that invest overseas, provide lower rates for industries with powerful lobbyists like the oil and gas industry, and allow tax shelters to proliferate. As President, Barack Obama will close the door to international tax havens and plug offshore tax loopholes, saving the United States tens of billions of dollars each year.

Simplify Tax Filings for Middle-Class Americans.

Barack Obama believes that the IRS has created a tax filing process that, for millions of Americans, is far too complicated for the filings they ultimately make. Deductions and exemptions are built into the system, but ordinary people don't have the time to figure them out without going to an expert preparer—yet another cost at tax time. In 2004, the IRS estimated that it took twenty-eight hours for an individual to complete his or her tax filing. As President, Barack Obama will dramatically simplify tax filings so that millions of Americans will be able to do their taxes in less than five minutes. An Obama Administration will ensure that the IRS uses the information it already gets from banks and employers to give taxpayers the option of prefilled tax forms to verify, sign, and return. According to expert estimates, this will save Americans up to two hundred million total hours of work and aggravation and up to $2 billion in tax preparer fees.

Create a Reserve Fund for Emergencies and Deficit Reduction.

One can never know what kind of emergency may occur that will require the help of the federal government. If we have no money put away for these possibilities, we run the risk of allowing these unforeseen events to cause even more economic pain and derail our long-term growth. That's why Barack Obama will not only pay for all his proposals, but also will put aside additional projected savings into an emergency reserve fund to meet any unexpected needs and reduce the deficit.

INVESTING
IN OUR PROSPERITY
Creating Our Economic Future

"Tomorrow's businesses won't just trade in goods or services; they'll deal in information. As Google has grown, I've seen just how easily the government can encourage or discourage innovation. Barack Obama's policies will help this country's next generation of companies flourish, and his proposals will give a child somewhere in America the tools and motivation to make the next great leap in technology."

—Vint Cerf

Vice President and Chief Internet Evangelist of Google and "Father of the Internet"

"We must break our nation's dangerous addiction to foreign oil. As an entrepreneur, I've invested heavily in alternative energy sources because I share Barack Obama's belief that we must work toward independence now before it's too late. His policies will encourage the development of ethanol, wind, solar, and other forms of alternative energy, and his proposals show a real dedication to achieving a clean energy future for ourselves and our children."

—Vinod Khosla

Cofounding CEO of Sun Microsystems and alternative energy expert

America's prosperity has always risen from the ground up. From the earliest days of our founding, it has been the hard work and ingenuity of our people that's served as the wellspring of our economic strength. But an entrepreneur can't nurture an idea into a business, a family can't prepare their kids for a good job, and a community can't grow and expand without the nation making investments in science, technology, and infrastructure and providing educational opportunities to our people. That's why we built the great land-grant universities as our nation expanded west, sent the Greatest Generation to college on the GI Bill, and invested in the science and research that have led to new discoveries and entire new industries. It's why the generations that came before us built the Erie Canal at the start of the nineteenth century, the transcontinental railroad after the Civil War, and the interstate highway system in the 1950s. And it's why we electrified rural America during the depths of the Great Depression and laid fiber optic cables in our own time. Investing in the future has been critical to making America competitive and creating high-paying jobs for our people. We've done it throughout our history, and it's what this country will do again when Barack Obama is President of the United States.

In a world where old boundaries are disappearing and where communication, connection, and competition can come from anywhere, it's even more important that the United States prepares for the future. We must make sure that the American people have the tools they need to thrive in a world that is more tightly linked, has more economic competition, and is facing new global challenges.

Many are anxious about this new world because they worry about the disruption it brings. But globalization and global economic competition cannot be stopped. It is the reality we are facing in this new century, with all its promise and possible pitfalls. Yet, if we take the right steps now, America can ride this wave of change, maintain its economic leadership in the twenty-first century, and create high-wage jobs for millions of Americans.

Barack Obama knows that America can compete—and succeed—in the twenty-first century, and that this success will depend on our government being as dynamic, determined, and innovative as the American people. We can neither shrink from the challenge of globalization nor fall back on the same tired and failed approaches of the last eight years. He knows that the right way to deal with the realities of the global economy is to shape them so that they benefit not the privileged few, but the hardworking families, small businesses, and communities that are the backbone of our nation. It's time for new policies that invest in the growth of our economy and create the jobs and opportunities of the future. As President, Barack Obama will pursue a competitiveness agenda built upon education and energy, innovation and infrastructure, trade and reform that will create jobs and prosperity for all Americans.

Promote Our Energy Independence and Create Five Million Green Jobs

Our dependence on foreign oil endangers our national security, imperils our planet, and harms our economy. Every single President since Richard Nixon has promised to do something to strengthen our energy independence and curb our use of Middle East oil and other fossil fuels, but we are more dependent on it than ever before. Now, as American families and businesses are stretched to the limit with high gas prices, we can no longer afford Washington's paralysis on this critical issue. As our climate warms and scientists predict more severe storms and severe weather that ruin crops, devastate cities, and destabilize whole regions, we must act now to wean ourselves off the fossil fuels that produce the greenhouse gases that cause global warming.

This will be a huge challenge, but it also is an equally large opportunity to make the United States the world leader in the green-energy industries of tomorrow. Already, our economic competitors are racing to dominate these new clean-energy industries and the jobs that come with them. The question is not whether a clean-energy economy is in our future; it's where it will thrive. Barack Obama wants it to thrive right here in the United States of America, and his plan to make our country more energy independent will develop these new industries and create five million new green jobs.

Barack Obama believes we have an economic, national security, and moral imperative to address our dependence on foreign oil and tackle climate change in a serious, sustainable manner. Barack Obama's comprehensive plan to combat global warming and achieve energy security will:

Increase Fuel Economy Standards.

As a Senator, Barack Obama developed an innovative approach to double fuel economy standards within eighteen years while protecting the financial future of domestic automakers. As President, he will work in partnership with our automakers, autoworkers, and suppliers to implement that plan and provide $4 billion in retooling tax credits and loan guarantees for domestic auto plants and parts manufacturers so that new fuel-efficient cars can be built in the United States rather than overseas. This measure will strengthen the U.S. manufacturing sector, help ensure that American workers will build the high-demand cars of the future, and help eliminate the need for the United States to import oil from the Middle East and Venezuela within ten years.

Get One Million Plug-in Electric Vehicles on the Road by 2015.

As a U.S. Senator, Barack Obama has led efforts to jumpstart federal investment in advanced vehicles, including combined plug-in hybrid/flexible-fuel vehicles, which can get more than 150 miles per gallon of gas. As President, Barack Obama will continue this leadership by investing in advanced vehicle technology with a specific focus on R&D in advanced battery technology. The increased federal funding will leverage private sector funds and support our domestic automakers to bring plug-in hybrids and other advanced vehicles to American consumers.

Cut Taxes for Drivers Who Buy Fuel-Efficient Automobiles.

Right now, there are waiting lists to buy fuel-efficient, hybrid cars. In addition, there are thousands more who would like to buy these cars and save money at the pump, but they can't afford the higher price. As President, Barack Obama will provide a $7,000 tax credit for the purchase of advanced technology vehicles, as well as conversion tax credits.

A "Use It or Lose It" Approach to Existing Leases.

Oil companies have access to 68 million acres of land, over 40 million offshore, in which they are not drilling. Drilling in open areas could significantly increase domestic oil and gas production. Barack Obama will require oil companies to diligently develop these leases or turn them over so that another company can develop them.

Promote the Responsible Domestic Production of Oil and Natural Gas.

An Obama Administration will set up a process for early identification of any infrastructure obstacles/shortages or possible federal permitting process delays to drilling in the

Bakken Shale in Montana and North Dakota, the Barnett Shale formation in Texas, the Fayetteville Shale in Arkansas, and the National Petroleum Reserve–Alaska (NPR-A).

Prioritize the Construction of the Alaska Natural Gas Pipeline.

As President, Barack Obama will work with the Canadian government, the state of Alaska, oil and gas producers, and other stakeholders to facilitate construction of the pipeline. While this pipeline was proposed in 1976, and Congress authorized up to $18 billion in loan guarantees for this project in 2004, there has been no progress in building this critical energy infrastructure under the Bush Administration. The planned pipeline would have a daily capacity of 4 billion cubic feet of natural gas, or almost 7 percent of current U.S. consumption. Not only is this pipeline critical to our energy security, it will create thousands of new jobs.

Create Five Million New Green Jobs.

With a President who sets a clean-energy goal for our nation, a clear carbon-emissions target, and smart investments, America can build a clean-energy future while creating five million new green jobs right here in the United States for our workers. Barack Obama will use some of the revenue generated from the cap-and-trade permit auction to invest in climate-friendly energy development and deployment. An Obama Administration will invest $150 billion over ten years to invest in clean energy, advance the next generation of biofuels and fuel infrastructure, accelerate the commercialization of plug-in hybrids, promote the development of

> *"I do believe that if all of us are willing to share the burdens and benefits of this new economy, then all of us will prosper . . . because we're willing to take responsibility as individuals to work harder and think more and innovate further."*
>
> —BARACK OBAMA, July 7, 2008, St. Louis, Missouri

commercial-scale renewable-energy projects, invest in low-emissions coal plants, and begin the transition to a new digital electricity grid. This will transform our economy and create five million new jobs in such areas as research, manufacturing, and construction while spurring the creation of new businesses. A principal focus of this fund will be devoted to ensuring that technologies that are developed in the United States are commercialized in the United States and deployed around the globe. As President, Barack Obama will:

- Double federal science and research funding for clean-energy projects including those that make use of our biomass, solar, and wind resources.
- Invest in job training and transition programs to help workers and industries adapt to clean-technology development and production.
- Work to ensure that advanced biofuels, including cellulosic ethanol, are developed and incorporated into our

national supply as soon as possible. An Obama Administration will set the goal of 2 billion gallons of cellulosic ethanol in our system by 2013.

- Rapidly develop and deploy clean coal technology. Barack Obama will direct his Secretary of Energy to enter public-private partnerships to build five commercial-scale carbon-capture and -sequestration facilities.
- Extend the federal Production Tax Credit (PTC) for five years to encourage the production of renewable energy, and ensure that nuclear energy is used with safety and security.
- Weatherize one million homes annually to help reduce energy costs for all.
- Set a goal to reduce electricity demand by 15 percent from projected levels by 2020.

Reduce Carbon Emissions 80 Percent by 2050.

Barack Obama is a champion of the national effort to cut greenhouse gas emissions. As President, Barack Obama will institute a market-based cap-and-trade system to reduce carbon emissions by the amount scientists say is necessary to avoid catastrophic change—80 percent below 1990 levels by 2050. He will start reducing emissions immediately in his Administration by establishing strong annual reduction targets, and he'll also implement a mandate of reducing emissions to 1990 levels by 2020. A cap-and-trade program draws on the power of the marketplace to reduce emissions in a cost-effective and flexible manner. Under the program, an overall cap on carbon emissions is established and then divided up into individual allowances that represent the permission to emit that amount. To ensure complete openness with the public and prevent unjustified corporate welfare, all allowances will be auctioned. Companies will be free to buy and sell allowances so that we can reduce pollution at the lowest cost, legacy producers will have the ability to adjust, and American innovators and entrepreneurs will have a direct incentive to find new ways to reduce pollution. The Obama plan would take a small portion of the auction receipts, $15 billion per year, and use it to make the critical investments to help improve energy efficiency, invest in alternative fuels, and take other measures to help the economy adjust. The remainder of the receipts would be reserved for rebates and other transition relief to help consumers and communities adjust to the new-energy economy.

Establish a National Low-Carbon Fuel Standard.

Barack Obama will establish a National Low-Carbon Fuel Standard (LCFS) to speed the introduction of low-carbon nonpetroleum fuels. The standard will require fuels suppliers to reduce the carbon their fuel emits by 10 percent by 2020.

Require 10 Percent of Electricity to Come from Renewable Sources by 2012.

As President, Barack Obama will require that 10 percent of electricity consumed in the United States is derived from clean, sustainable energy sources, like solar, wind, and geothermal, by 2012. This requirement will spur significant private-sector investment in renewable sources of energy and create thousands of new American jobs, especially in rural areas. And Barack Obama believes that the federal government, the nation's largest consumer of energy, must take the lead. As President, he will ensure that at least 30 percent of the federal government's electricity comes from renewable sources by 2020.

Make the Federal Government the Leader in Saving Electricity.

Barack Obama believes that the federal government should take the lead in reducing its energy consumption. As President, he will ensure that all new federal buildings produce zero emissions by 2025, and to help reach that goal, he will ensure that all new federal buildings are 40 percent more efficient within the next five years.

Use Innovative Measures to Dramatically Improve Efficiency of Buildings.

Buildings account for nearly 40 percent of carbon emissions in the United States today, and carbon emissions from buildings are expected to grow faster than emissions from other major parts of our economy. It is expected that fifteen million new buildings will be constructed between today and 2015. Barack Obama believes that we have both an opportunity and a responsibility to make our new and existing buildings more efficient consumers of electricity; as President, he will establish a goal of making all new buildings carbon neutral, or produce zero emissions, by 2030. He will also establish a national goal of improving new-building efficiency by 50 percent and existing-building efficiency by 25 percent over the next decade to help us meet the 2030 goal. To do this, he will create a competitive grant program to award those states and local communities that take the first steps in implementing new building codes that prioritize energy efficiency, and he will provide early adopter grants and other financial assistance to states that "flip" the incentives to utilities by ensuring companies get increased profits for improving energy efficiency, rather than higher energy consumption.

Invest in a Digital Smart Grid.

Like other pieces of infrastructure, such as roads and bridges, our energy grid is outdated and inefficient, resulting in $50–100 billion losses to the U.S. economy each year. The 2003 East Coast blackout alone resulted in a $10 billion economic loss. Like President Eisenhower did with the interstate highway system, Barack Obama will pursue a major investment in our national utility grid to enable a tremendous increase in renewable generation and accommodate twenty-first-century energy requirements, such as reliability, smart metering, and distributed storage. An Obama Administration will invest federal money to leverage additional state and private sector funds to help create a digitally connected power grid. Installing a smart grid will help consumers produce electricity at home through solar panels or wind turbines, and allow them to sell electricity back through the grid for other consumers. This will help consumers reduce their energy use during peak hours when electricity is more expensive.

Build More Livable and Sustainable Communities.

As President, Barack Obama will ensure that smart growth considerations are taken into account in the federal transportation funding process. He will promote greater bicycle and pedestrian usage of roads and sidewalks, and he will also recommit federal resources to public mass transportation projects across the country. Barack Obama will also reform the tax code to make benefits for driving and public transit or ridesharing equal.

Restore U.S. Leadership and Rally the World to Stop Global Warming.

The United States must regain its leadership role in confronting the threat of climate change. Barack Obama will immediately make clear that under his leadership, there will be a swift and dramatic change in America's willingness to work with our global partners to bring about a new-energy future. He will signal to the world the U.S. commitment to climate change leadership by implementing an aggressive domestic cap-and-trade program combined with increased investments in clean-energy development and deployment. He will call for a Global Energy Forum (including all G-8 members plus Brazil, China, India, Mexico, and South Africa) of the world's largest emitters to focus exclusively on global energy and environmental issues. This Global Energy Forum will complement—and ultimately merge with—the much larger negotiation process underway at the UN to develop a post-Kyoto framework. Barack Obama also will:

- Re-engage with the diplomatic efforts under the UN Framework Convention on Climate Change, the main international forum dedicated to addressing the climate problem.
- Create a Technology Transfer program within the De-

partment of Energy dedicated to exporting climate-friendly technologies, including green buildings, clean coal, and advanced automobiles, to developing countries to help them combat climate change.

- Use existing organizations, like NATO, to make energy security a shared global goal.
- Offer incentives to farmers and ranchers abroad to maintain forests and manage them sustainably.

A World-Class Education for Every American

Ensuring America's competitive edge in the twenty-first century starts with investing in our workers by providing every American the opportunity to get a world-class education from cradle through to adulthood. We know that in this global economy, countries that out educate us today will outcompete us tomorrow. Whether they are conservative or liberal, Republican or Democrat, every economist agrees that in this digital age, a highly educated and skilled workforce will be critical not only to individual opportunity, but to the overall success of our economy as well.

Yet only 20 percent of American students are prepared to take college classes in English, math, and science. We have one of the highest dropout rates of any industrialized nation, and barely one-tenth of our low-income students will graduate from college. China is already graduating four times as many engineers as we do, and our share of twenty-four-year-olds with college degrees now falls somewhere between

Bulgaria and Costa Rica. This is morally unacceptable and economically untenable.

Barack Obama believes that providing a high-quality education is key to addressing many of our country's challenges, and that world-class public schools provide the path to global opportunity, high-quality employment, and strong local communities. While we have many good schools in America, we can still do a better job educating our children and scaling up successful programs so that they are the norm across the country. We must set ambitious goals for education that include advanced twenty-first-century skills, good character, and informed citizenship. It's time to make a historic commitment to education—a real commitment that will require new resources and new reforms. As President, Barack Obama will:

Bring Responsibility and Values to Our Classrooms.

Barack Obama will call on parents, families, and schools to work together and take responsibility for instilling in young people our best shared values, like honesty, hard work, and good citizenship. A society has not succeeded if we prepare our young people for academic success but have not developed their values and readiness for responsible citizenship. As President, Barack Obama will:

- Require every school receiving federal funding to lay out clear and high expectations for student behavior and shared values, agreed on by the school's educators and parents.
- Encourage schools and parents to work together to

establish a school-family contract laying out expectations for student attendance, behavior, and homework.
- Call on parents to turn off the TV and video games, make sure their children are getting their homework done, and work to take a greater stake in their child's education both in and outside of school.
- Expect all students to engage in community service.

Invest in Zero-to-Five Early Childhood Education.

Research shows that early experiences shape whether or not a child's brain develops strong skills for future learning, behavior, and success. Investing in early childhood education during the infant and toddler years is particularly critical. For every dollar invested in high-quality, comprehensive programs supporting children and families from birth, there is a $7 to $10 return to society in decreased need for special education services, higher graduation and employment rates, less crime, less use of the public welfare system, and better health. Though parents remain the first teachers for our children, an increasing number of infants and toddlers spend significant parts of their day with caretakers other than their parents. In addition to ensuring that child care is accessible and affordable, we must do more to ensure that it is of a high quality and provides the early-education experiences our children need. Barack Obama has a comprehensive "Zero to Five" plan that will provide critical supports to young children and their parents by investing $10 billion per year to:

- Establish Early Learning Challenge Grants to enable states to create or expand high-quality early-care and education programs for pregnant women and early care, as well as voluntary, universal preschool for all children.

- Quadruple the number of eligible children for Early Head Start, increase Head Start funding, and improve quality for both.
- Create a Presidential Early Learning Council to increase collaboration and program coordination across federal, state, and local levels.
- Provide affordable and high-quality child care by expanding the Child and Dependent Care Tax Credit, ensuring adequate funding for the Child Care Development Block Grant (CCDBG) program, and supporting efforts to develop quality rating systems for child care that reflect higher standards and to support teacher and staff training as well as professional development.

Improve Accountability and Reform No Child Left Behind.

Barack Obama believes that the overall goal of the No Child Left Behind Act (NCLB) is the right one—ensuring that all children can meet high standards—but the law has significant flaws that need to be addressed. He believes it was wrong to force teachers, principals, and schools to accomplish the goals of No Child Left Behind without the necessary resources. NCLB has demoralized our educators, broken its promise to our children, and must be changed in a fundamental way. As President, he will improve the assessments used to track student progress so that we provide educators and students with timely feedback about how to improve student learning, measure readiness for college and success in an information-age workplace, and show whether individual students are making progress toward reaching high standards.

Recruit, Prepare, Retain, and Reward America's Teachers.

From the moment our children step into a classroom, the single most important factor in determining how well they learn is their teacher. Barack Obama values teachers and the central role that they play in education. To ensure competent, effective teachers in schools that are organized for success, Barack Obama will:

- Create substantial, sustained Teaching Service Scholarships that completely cover training costs in high-quality teacher-preparation or alternative-certification programs at the undergraduate or graduate level for those who are willing to teach in a high-need field or location for at least four years.
- Require professional accreditation of all programs preparing teachers, with a focus on evidence regarding how well teachers are prepared to meet the challenges of their demanding jobs.
- Develop a performance test that measures actual teaching skill in content areas, which will do more than merely measure basic skills and subject matter knowledge but will collect evidence about how prospective teachers plan and teach in the classroom, evaluate student work, and adapt their teaching to student learning needs.
- Provide $100 million to stimulate teacher education reforms with Professional Development Schools that,

like teaching hospitals in medicine, enable teachers to learn from expert practitioners in the field by partnering universities with school sites.

- Create slots for 30,000 exceptionally well-prepared teacher recruits to go to high-need schools to provide long-term commitment and leadership in these districts through his Teaching Residency Programs.

- Provide mentoring for beginning teachers so that more of them stay in teaching and develop sophisticated skills.

- Create incentives for shared planning and learning time for teachers.

- Establish a Career Ladder Initiative that would support higher compensation for teachers in school districts that provide ongoing professional development and reward accomplished teachers for deep knowledge of subjects, additional skills, and excelling in the classroom.

- Continue to support innovation and experimentation in teaching—by adapting school curricula and the school calendar to the needs of the twenty-first century; by updating the schools of education that produce most of our teachers; by welcoming charter schools within the public schools system; and by streamlining the certification process for engineers or businesspeople who want to shift careers and teach.

Support School Principals.

Principals are integral to the success of a school. Yet national studies suggest that there is a growing shortage of well-prepared school principals even while the demands of principalship are growing. School leaders today need not only to

> *"I believe it's time to lead a new era of mutual responsibility in education—one where we all come together for the sake of our children's success."*
>
> —BARACK OBAMA, May 28, 2008, Thornton, Colorado

manage schools, they need to develop high-quality instruction and professional development and redesign school organizations so that they better support student and teacher learning. As President, Barack Obama will create a challenge grant program for states and districts in order to provide funding for the creation or enhancement of state leadership academies and encourage principals to grow professionally over the course of their careers.

Encourage Additional Learning Time.

The typical school day is a throwback to America's agricultural era and is not on par with that of other developed countries around the world. We expect students to learn more today than ever before and many experts agree that additional learning time, particularly for struggling students, is important to gaining knowledge and skills for the twenty-first century. Longer school days or longer school years can help provide additional learning time for students to close the achievement gap. An Obama Administration will create a $200 million grant program for states and districts that want to provide additional learning time for students in need.

Reduce the High School Dropout Rate.

Only 70 percent of U.S. high school students graduate with a diploma. Today, dropouts are twice as likely to be unemployed; those who do work earn less, have bleaker career prospects, and often lack health insurance. As President, Barack Obama will work to reduce the dropout rate by providing federal support to improve the education of students in the crucial middle grades, develop more small schools, and back alternative education pathways that work.

Double Funding for After-School Opportunities.

Expanding access to high-quality after-school programs will help children learn and strengthen a broad range of skills as well as provide relief to working parents who have to juggle child care and work responsibilities. As President, Barack Obama will double funding for the main federal support for after-school programs, the 21st Century Community Learning Centers Program, to serve one million more children each year. He will also expand summer learning opportunities to serve an additional one million children each year.

Support English Language Learners.

Barack Obama supports transitional bilingual education and will help Limited English Proficient students get ahead by supporting and funding English Language Learner (ELL) classes. He will support development of appropriate assessments for ELL students, monitor the progress of students learning English, and hold schools accountable for making sure these students complete school.

Make College Affordable for Everyone.

A college education is increasingly vital for success in the American economy, yet college costs have grown nearly 40 percent in the past five years. If we do not act now, by 2010, it's estimated that over the previous ten years, two million academically qualified students will not go to college because they can't afford it. As President, Barack Obama will work to make college affordable and ensure the dream of college is accessible for all Americans. He will:

- Create a new $4,000 American Opportunity Tax Credit, a fully refundable credit that will make community college completely free and cover two-thirds the cost of tuition at the average public college or university for those willing to perform 100 hours a year of public service.
- Simplify and streamline the onerous financial aid application process that too often stands in the way of getting aid for college.
- Increase the maximum limit for Pell Grants for low-income students so it keeps pace with the cost of living.
- Create a Community College Partnership Program that will help community colleges provide the types of skills, degrees, and technical education that are in high demand from students and local industry and reward those colleges that increase their numbers of transfer students to four-year institutions.
- Eliminate federal subsidies to private student loan companies.

Expand Opportunities for Lifelong Learning.

To succeed in the new economy, workers will have to continually update their skills to keep pace with change. No longer can education stop at high school, technical school, or college; it must be for a lifetime. As President, Barack Obama will reauthorize the Workforce Investment Act, increase funding for vocational and technical education, and support efforts by unions to develop and administer workforce development programs. An Obama Administration also will help workers learn the skills to take the green jobs of tomorrow and provide grants to turn community colleges' computer centers into true community resources.

Make America the Undisputed Leader in Science and Technology

In the past, government funding for scientific research has yielded innovations that have improved the landscape of American life—technologies like the Internet, digital photography, Global Positioning System technology, laser surgery, and chemotherapy. Today, we face a new set of challenges, including energy security and climate change. Yet, the United States is losing its scientific dominance. Among industrialized nations, our country's scores on international science and math tests rank in the bottom third and bottom fifth, respectively. Over the last three decades, federal funding for the physical, mathematical, and engineering sciences has declined at a time when other countries are substantially increasing their own research budgets. Yet, more than 80 percent of the fastest-growing occupations are dependent upon a knowledge base in science and math, and some economists estimate that about one half of U.S. economic growth since World War II has been the result of technological innovation.

Barack Obama believes that to create widespread prosperity, America cannot lose its technological edge. He is committed to investing in and empowering a new generation of twenty-first-century innovators and ensuring that they have the resources they need to compete in the global economy while helping create new jobs and new opportunities for American workers. As President, he will:

Deploy the Next-Generation Broadband.

The United States once led the world in broadband deployment; now we rank fifteenth. Barack Obama believes that must change, and as President will work to put America back on top when it comes to broadband penetration and Internet access. As a country, we have ensured that every American has access to telephone service and electricity, regardless of economic status, and Barack Obama will do likewise for broadband Internet access. An Obama Administration will bring true broadband to every community in America by reforming the Universal Service Fund; unleashing the nation's wireless spectrum; and bringing broadband to our schools, libraries, and hospitals.

Protect the Openness of the Internet.

A key reason the Internet has been such a success is because it is the most open network in history. Barack Obama believes that it needs to stay that way. He strongly supports the principle of network neutrality to preserve the benefits of open competition on the Internet. Users must be free to access content, to use applications, and to attach personal devices, and receive accurate and honest information about service plans. In addition, Barack Obama will encourage diversity in the ownership of broadcast media, promote the development of new media outlets for expression of diverse viewpoints, and clarify the public-interest obligations of broadcasters who occupy the nation's spectrum.

Safeguard Privacy.

Barack Obama will strengthen privacy protections for the digital age and will harness the power of technology to hold government and business accountable for violations of personal privacy. He will do this by increasing the Federal Trade Commission's enforcement budget, stepping up international cooperation to track down cyber-criminals, and ensuring that e-health records and powerful databases containing information on Americans that are necessary tools in the fight against terrorism are not misused. Barack Obama also will support efforts to empower parents to guide what their children do and see online. As President, Barack Obama will encourage the creation of Public Media 2.0., the next generation of public media that will create the *Sesame Street* of the digital age and other video and interactive programming that educates and informs. He will also help parents protect their children from Internet predators and the hateful messages and graphic violence and sex that are sometimes part of the online world.

Double Federal Funding for Basic Scientific Research.

As a share of the Gross Domestic Product, American federal investment in the physical sciences and engineering research has dropped by half since 1970. To foster home-grown innovation, help ensure the competitiveness of U.S. technology-based businesses, and ensure that twenty-first-century jobs can and will grow in America, Barack Obama will double federal funding for basic research. He also will back investments in biomedical research, medical education, and training in health-related fields, through the National Institutes of Health and the National Science Foundation, including doubling funding for cancer research. In addition, as President, Barack Obama will make the Research and Experimentation tax credit permanent to give businesses the certainty they need to make long-term investments in domestic research and development.

Advance Stem Cell Research.

Despite recent advances pointing to alternatives like adult stem cell and cord blood, embryonic stem cells remain unmatched in their potential for treatment of a wide variety of diseases and health conditions. Barack Obama has been a long-term supporter of increased stem cell research, and as President, he will allow greater federal government funding on a wider array of stem cell lines.

Upgrade Math and Science Education.

Educating students who excel in math and science at every level is critical to the competitiveness of our nation. As

President, Barack Obama will emphasize the importance of technology literacy, ensuring that all public school children are equipped with the necessary science, technology, and math skills to succeed in the twenty-first-century economy. He will fight for access to computers and broadband connections in public schools along with qualified teachers, engaging curricula, and a commitment to developing skills in the field of technology. Barack Obama's Teaching Service Scholarship Program will prioritize recruiting math, science, and technology degree graduates to become teachers. An Obama Administration will work to increase our number of science and engineering graduates, encourage undergraduates studying math and science to pursue graduate studies, and work to increase the representation of minorities and women in the science and technology pipeline, tapping the diversity of America to meet the increasing demand for a skilled workforce.

Appoint a National Chief Technology Officer.

Barack Obama will use technology to reform government and improve the exchange of information between the federal government and citizens while ensuring the security of our networks. To that end, he will appoint the nation's first Chief Technology Officer (CTO) to ensure that our government and all its agencies have the right infrastructure, policies, and services for the twenty-first century. The CTO will ensure the safety of our networks and will lead an interagency effort, working with chief technology and chief information officers of each of the federal agencies to ensure that they use best-in-class technologies and share best practices.

Reform the Patent System.

A system that produces timely, high-quality patents is essential for global competitiveness in the twenty-first century. As President, Barack Obama will ensure that our patent laws protect legitimate rights while not stifling innovation and collaboration. He will give the Patent and Trademark Office (PTO) the resources to improve patent quality and open up the patent process to citizen input.

Build the Infrastructure of the Twenty-first Century

A century ago, Teddy Roosevelt called together leaders from business and government to develop a plan for a twentieth-century infrastructure. Fifty years ago, Republican Dwight Eisenhower and Democrat Al Gore, Sr., worked together to build the Interstate Highway System. Today, however, too many of our nation's railways, highways, bridges, airports, and neighborhood streets are slowly decaying due to lack of investment and strategic long-term planning. As our society becomes more mobile and interconnected, the need for twenty-first-century transportation networks has never been greater. As our economy slows, repairing and upgrading our infrastructure is an effective way to revive it and create new jobs. In the longer term, infrastructure investment will enable the United States to compete with the rest of the world and keep good jobs here at home. After all, in this day and age, businesses can now locate just about anywhere in the world and bring the jobs they create with them—and a modern infrastructure is critical to ensuring that those jobs come to and stay in America. As President, Barack Obama will make strengthening our transportation systems—including our roads and bridges—and building a world-class, twenty-first-century infrastructure a top priority. He will:

Create a National Infrastructure Reinvestment Bank.

To expand and enhance federal transportation investments, Barack Obama will create a new National Infrastructure Reinvestment Bank. To get away from the legacy of wasteful, earmarked spending that has given us the system we have today, this will be an independent entity directed by non-political experts on our national needs. The bank will invest in our nation's most challenging transportation infrastructure needs, including intermodal transport capacities. The bank will receive an infusion of federal money, $6 billion per year, and cooperate with private funding sources to provide billions more in financing for transportation infrastructure projects across the nation. These projects will lead to the creation of up to two million new jobs per year and stimulate approximately $35 billion per year in new economic activity.

Improve and Modernize Air Traffic Control.

Because of an outdated air-traffic control system and over-scheduling at airports already operating at full capacity, there were a record number of flight delays during the first half of 2007. In 2006, there were nearly 1,100 fewer air traffic controllers working in U.S. air traffic facilities than three years prior, despite increasing air traffic. Barack Obama will work with Congress to modernize the nation's air traffic

> *"Years from now, we could drive on new roads, depend on safe bridges and stronger levees, and connect our cities with high-speed rail . . . That's what we must do to make sure that America runs on a strong, fair, and efficient foundation."*
>
> —BARACK OBAMA, June 26, 2007, Pittsburgh, Pennsylvania

control system, and he will direct the new FAA Administrator to work cooperatively with the frontline air traffic controllers to restore morale and improve working conditions and operations at the agency.

Strengthen Airline Safety and Regulations.

Over the past several months there have been reports that FAA leadership ignored warnings from its employees that too many commercial planes failed to meet federal safety guidelines. As a result of FAA whistleblowers coming to the public with this information, there have been widespread groundings of commercial planes, which have added considerable strain to our airline industry. Barack Obama believes that we must restore competence, independence, and credibility to the FAA. As President, he will appoint a qualified FAA Administrator who will not play politics with the safety of American travelers, and he will work with Congress to strengthen the FAA's mandate.

Support Amtrak Funding and the Development of High-Speed Rail.

In many parts of the country, Amtrak is the only form of reliable intercity transportation. Barack Obama strongly supports federal financial support for Amtrak, and believes we need to reform Amtrak to improve accountability. As President, Barack Obama will continue to fight for Amtrak funding and reform—as well as new high-speed rail—so that individuals, families, and businesses throughout the country have safe and reliable transportation options.

Invest in Public Transportation.

Public transit not only reduces the amount of time individuals spend commuting, but also has significant benefits to air quality, public health, and reducing greenhouse gas emissions. Barack Obama will recommit federal resources to public mass transportation projects across the country and will work with state and local governments on efforts to create new, effective public transportation systems and modernize our aging urban public transit infrastructure. Barack Obama also will reform the tax code so that tax benefits that go to commuters are equal between those who drive and those who take public transportation.

Help Our Small Businesses and Manufacturers Thrive and Create Jobs

Small businesses are the engines of job growth in America, creating, on average, more than two-thirds of new jobs each year. These jobs are more likely to stay here in the United States, anchoring families and communities across the country. Yet small businesses and manufacturers are being hammered by the high cost of health care and energy, along with a slowing economy. Often, they have trouble finding the capital and expertise they need to grow, and they don't have the power and connections that their big competitors can use. If we expect to compete and succeed in the global economy, our nation can't afford to have our entrepreneurs' best ideas never become reality. As President, Barack Obama will improve the business climate for small businesses and manufacturers and help lay the foundations for them to create good new jobs that will stay here in the United States. He will:

Eliminate Capital Gains Taxes and Provide New Health Care Tax Cuts for Small Businesses.

To provide meaningful tax relief to small businesses, while encouraging innovation and job creation, Barack Obama will eliminate all capital gains taxes on start-up and small businesses. He also will provide a new 50 percent tax credit for small firms that offer quality health care to their employees. As President, Barack Obama also will work to expand federal lending to small businesses and will create a new national network of public-private business incubators to facilitate the work of entrepreneurs in creating start-up companies. Finally, recognizing that less than 1 percent of the $250 billion in venture capital dollars invested annually nationwide has been directed to the country's 4.4 million minority business owners, an Obama Administration will strengthen Small Business Administration programs that provide capital to minority-owned businesses, support outreach programs that help minority business owners apply for loans, and work to encourage the growth and capacity of minority firms.

Support Rural Economic Development.

Small business creates most of the new jobs and self-employment opportunities in rural America. To spur the development of small business and value-added agriculture, an Obama Administration will increase funding for the Value Added Producer Grant Program, which provides capital for farmers to create value-added enterprises, such as cooperative marketing initiatives for high-value crops and livestock and farmer-owned processing plants. He also will provide training and technical assistance for rural small businesses, and provide a 20 percent tax credit on up to $50,000 of investment in small owner-operated businesses. Barack Obama also will provide a capital gains tax break for landowners selling to family farmers just starting out, and a first-time buyers' tax credit for new farmers.

Spur Regional Economic Growth.

From North Carolina's Research Triangle to Nashville's thriving entertainment cluster, innovation and economic growth is found not just in one city or county, but in entire metropolitan regions. As President, Barack Obama will support innovation clusters—regional centers of innovation and next-generation industries—across the country. He will provide grants both for planning these clusters and cultivating their growth. Matching grants will assist states with a variety of activities, including building research parks, running workforce attraction efforts, supporting regional transportation projects tied to developing clusters, and bolstering local job training.

Invest in Next-Generation Manufacturing Innovation.

Manufacturing supports one-in-six jobs in the nation, and pays average wages and benefits that are 23 percent higher than the rest of the economy. Yet under President Bush, America has lost 3.7 million manufacturing jobs, a 21 percent decline. This decline has not only cost jobs, but also threatens America's status as a leading innovator. As President, Barack Obama will invest in manufacturing by doubling funding for the Manufacturing Extension Partnership—an innovative program that works with manufacturers across the country to improve efficiency, implement new technology, and strengthen company growth. Barack Obama also will create an Advanced Manufacturing Fund to identify and invest in the most compelling advanced manufacturing strategies.

Convert Our Manufacturing Centers into Clean Technology Leaders.

America boasts the highest-skilled manufacturing workforce and advanced manufacturing facilities in the world, both of which have powered economic growth in America for decades. Barack Obama believes that American companies and workers should build the high-demand technologies of the future, and he will help nurture America's success in clean-technology manufacturing by establishing a federal investment program to help manufacturing centers modernize and help Americans learn the new skills they need to produce green products. This federal grant program will allocate money to the states to identify and support local manufacturers with the most compelling plans for modernizing existing or closed manufacturing facilities to produce new advanced clean technologies. This investment will help provide the critical, up-front capital needed by small and midsize manufacturers to produce these innovative new technologies. Along with an increased federal investment in the research, development, and deployment of advanced technologies, this $1 billion per year investment will help spur sustainable economic growth in communities across the country.

Compete and Thrive in the Global Economy

Barack Obama is committed to ensuring that our international economic policies promote our values and the jobs and incomes of our workers. He understands that America is at its best when we embrace the global economy and open markets for our goods and services, while ensuring that we can compete on a level playing field. Yet, too often our trade agreements have been written to serve special interests with little focus on what will work best for our communities and working families. A failure to enforce our trade agreements and ensure that countries like China play by the rules has led to unnecessary job loss for countless American workers and devastation for too many communities.

It does not have to be this way. Barack Obama understands that while we have no choice but to embrace the global economy, we have the choice to change the policies of the last eight years to ensure that our trade and international economic policies are structured in a way that raises the aspirations and dignity of workers here and abroad, and does not initiate a race to the bottom that compromises the environment, the wages and rights of workers, and the competitiveness of our country. As President, Barack Obama will:

Open Up Foreign Markets to Support Good American Jobs.

Barack Obama believes trade agreements should open markets for the goods and services provided by our workers while ensuring that we are promoting strong labor and environmental standards around the world. When agreements meet those standards, Barack Obama will move forward on trade. When there are agreements like the Central American Free Trade Agreement that allow other countries to unfairly continue to protect their markets from our exports, he will stand firm against them. As President, Barack Obama will ensure that, once again, we have an Administration that is willing to use the World Trade Organization to enforce trade agreements and stop countries from giving unfair government subsidies to their own exporters and from using non-tariff barriers to block imports from the United States. He will fight for stronger protections for U.S. intellectual property and against counterfeiters. In the case of China, in particular, he will push for an end to an artificially devalued currency that puts U.S. companies at a perpetual disadvantage, and he will end imports of products that are dangerous to our children or families. American workers should be competing on a level playing field, and countries like China shouldn't be allowed to break the rules.

Help Workers Displaced by Trade and Globalization.

To help all workers adapt to a rapidly changing economy, Barack Obama will modernize and expand the existing system of Trade Adjustment Assistance (TAA) to include all workers hurt by changing trade patterns—including those in the service sector and those losing jobs going to countries with which we do not have trade agreements, such as China and India. He will create flexible education accounts that workers can use to retrain, provide retraining assistance for workers in sectors of the economy vulnerable to dislocation before they lose their jobs, and provide additional assistance for workers to afford health care. He will also sign into law an updated WARN Act that requires large employers to notify employees of a layoff ninety days before a plant closing—an increase of thirty days from today's standard. And he will expand and fully fund apprenticeship programs to help workers get credentials and skills in crafts that reward that investment with a middle-class income and benefits.

End Tax Breaks for Companies That Send Jobs Overseas.

Barack Obama believes that we should not be providing billions of dollars in tax incentives to companies to send their operations overseas, hide their profits in tax havens, or move their headquarters abroad to avoid paying U.S. taxes. We should take that money and reward companies that are creating jobs and investing here at home. As President, he will end tax breaks for companies that send jobs overseas, and will fight to ensure that public contracts are awarded to companies that are committed to American workers.

Reward Companies That Invest in America.

Barack Obama believes that we need to encourage companies to do their investing in America. As President, he will cut corporate taxes for companies that start or expand their operations in the United States to create jobs here. He believes that thousands of companies want to grow their businesses here at home and that we ought to make it as easy and as encouraging as possible for them to do that.

Strengthen Trade Enforcement to Protect American Jobs.

To compete in the world economy, American workers need a level playing field where the rules of the road are enforced fairly and evenly. As President, Barack Obama will take trade enforcement seriously. He will make it the top priority of the U.S. Trade Representative (USTR) Office, and he will increase resources for the USTR so it can carry out its responsibility to protect American interests. As President, Barack Obama will also negotiate only trade agreements that will benefit American workers and that have strong and enforceable labor and environmental standards in the body of the agreement.

Amend the North American Free Trade Agreement.

Barack Obama will work with the leaders of Canada and Mexico to fix the North American Free Trade Agreement (NAFTA) so that it works for American workers. NAFTA was oversold; it has not created the jobs and wealth that were promised. Barack Obama believes that we can, and must, make trade work for American workers by opening up foreign markets to U.S. goods and putting strong labor and environmental standards in the core of the agreement. As President, he will work to amend NAFTA so that it lives up to those important principles.

REBUILDING
AMERICA'S LEADERSHIP
Restoring Our Place in the World

"The qualities of an individual that allow him or her to lead can include experience, and Senator Obama has served admirably on the Senate Foreign Relations Committee. But the most important qualities of a good leader are integrity, character, and judgment.

These are the qualities we need in our next President. In my naval career I have had the opportunity to assess many men and women on their potential to lead in times of peace, war, or crisis. Senator Barack Obama is a leader. He will lead America well."

—Admiral John Nathman

United States Navy (Retired)

"Barack Obama's foreign policy is pragmatic, visionary, and tough. He understands the urgent need for American leadership in confronting many of the challenges ahead, first and foremost defending the safety and security of the American people. He will work with our friends and allies. Barack Obama will strengthen our ability to use all the tools of American power, and relentlessly promote the American values of freedom and justice for all people."

—Lee Hamilton

Former Chairman of the House Committee on Foreign Affairs and Vice-Chairman of the 9/11 Commission

Throughout our history, the greatest threats to our security came from distant countries separated from the American mainland by vast oceans. A strong and able military, supported by diplomacy at the highest levels; nimble intelligence services; and unparalleled economic power kept us safe.

In this new century, our open, interdependent world that makes it so easy to do business, travel, or communicate with people all over the globe also makes us vulnerable to new threats and security challenges. As we learned on September 11, a small band of terrorists has the ability to kill thousands of civilians innocently going about their lives. Dangerous weapons, including nuclear materials, could fall into the hands of terrorists. Programmers sitting in their local coffee shop could launch cyber attacks on the Pentagon, the CIA, or key parts of our infrastructure. A small nation thousands of miles away which slips into chaos and anarchy could become a failed state that incubates terrorists and regional conflict. An outbreak of a deadly infectious disease in a rural, undeveloped corner of the world can quickly make its way to our biggest cities.

While we recognize that this is a time of new peril, we must not forget that it is also a time of immense promise. With the right leadership, we can rebuild our alliances and rally the world to tackle these truly transnational challenges, replace despair with hope, and keep America secure, prosperous, and free.

To seize this moment in our nation's history, the old solutions will not do. An outdated mind-set which believes that we can overcome these challenges by fighting the last war will not make America safe and secure. It's time for new leadership for a changing world—for a President who understands the unconventional challenges we face and who can lead us to overcome these threats.

As a U.S. Senator, Barack Obama worked with Republican Senator Richard Lugar to enact a law to secure loose weapons and nuclear materials from terrorists. He opposed the war in Iraq from the start, arguing that it would distract us from defeating the real threat of Al Qaeda in Afghanistan. And he has worked to support our troops and veterans, combat deadly diseases around the world, free us from foreign oil, and stop climate change that can destabilize entire regions of the world.

As President, Barack Obama will turn the page on the failed ideology and tired thinking of the past and offer a tough, smart, and principled national security strategy that uses all elements of American power—military, diplomatic, and economic—to protect our nation. He will end the war in Iraq responsibly; finish the fight against Al Qaeda and the Taliban; prepare the military for the threats of the twenty-first century; secure all nuclear weapons and materials from terrorists and rogue states; achieve true energy security; and rebuild our alliances to restore our standing in the world and meet the challenges of our time.

End the War in Iraq Responsibly

Barack Obama opposed the war in Iraq in 2002 because he believed that while Saddam Hussein's Iraq was a horrible regime, it posed no immediate threat to the United States. He argued, instead, that we should "finish the fight with bin Laden and Al Qaeda." He warned that an invasion of Iraq would fan the flames of extremism in the Middle East and distract us from the fight against those responsible for the attacks of September 11.

Since that time, our men and women in uniform have done their jobs in Iraq with unparalleled bravery and courage. They have completed every mission we have given them. But over the past five and a half years, the United States has lost thousands of precious lives, spent more than half a trillion dollars, alienated allies, and neglected critical threats to our national security—particularly the war in Afghanistan against the Taliban and Al Qaeda.

As President, Barack Obama will lead our country in a new direction—responsibly ending the war in Iraq and redirecting our attention to Afghanistan and the pressing threats we face. He believes that now is the time for a responsible redeployment of our combat troops that pushes Iraq's leaders toward taking responsibility for their own problems, rebuilds our military, and refocuses our attention on defeating Al Qaeda and the Taliban. Barack Obama will:

Begin a Responsible, Phased Withdrawal.

Barack Obama believes that we need to be as careful getting out of Iraq as we were careless getting in. Immediately upon taking office, Barack Obama will give his Secretary of Defense and military commanders a new mission in Iraq: ending this war. Barack Obama agrees with military experts that we can safely redeploy our combat brigades at a pace that removes them in sixteen months' time. After this redeployment, Barack Obama will keep a residual force in Iraq to perform limited missions: targeting any remnants of Al Qaeda in Iraq; force protection; and training Iraqi Security Forces, so long as the Iraqis make political progress. An Obama Administration will not build permanent bases in Iraq.

Launch a Diplomatic Surge.

To reach a comprehensive compact on the stability of Iraq and the region, Barack Obama will launch an aggressive diplomatic effort. This effort will include all of Iraq's neighbors, including Iran and Syria, as suggested by the report of the bipartisan Iraq Study Group. This compact will aim to secure Iraq's borders; keep neighboring countries from meddling inside Iraq; isolate Al Qaeda; support reconciliation among Iraq's sectarian groups; and provide financial support for Iraq's reconstruction and development.

Prevent a Humanitarian Crisis.

While the bulk of our troops are redeployed, it does not mean that the United States will turn its back on the people of Iraq. Barack Obama believes that America has both a moral obligation and a national interest in confronting Iraq's humanitarian crisis. As President, he will form an international working group and dedicate $2 billion to help the more than five million Iraqi refugees throughout the region. Barack Obama will also work with Iraqi authorities and the international community to hold accountable the perpetrators of potential war crimes, crimes against humanity, and genocide. He will reserve the right to intervene militarily, with our international partners, to suppress genocidal violence within Iraq. Barack Obama also will press the Iraqi government, awash in oil revenue, to fairly and equitably distribute government revenues to meet the needs of the Iraqi people.

Finish the Fight Against Al Qaeda and Turn the Tide Against Global Terrorism

The attacks of September 11 were heinous acts that forced us to recognize that in this new century, we are no longer protected by our own power alone. In a globalized world, the power to destroy can stem from asymmetric threats such as individuals and terrorist groups with powerful weapons—not just states with armies.

Unfortunately, the Bush-Cheney Administration offered a twentieth-century response to this twenty-first-century problem and gave the terrorists the battle they want us to fight: a misguided invasion of Iraq, a nation that had nothing to do with the attacks of September 11. This, in turn, has tied down our military, stretched our budgets, increased the pool of terrorist recruits, and prompted the American people to question our engagement in the world. At the same time, instead of fighting Al Qaeda and its allies where they are located and on the wider battlefield of ideas, the leaders in Washington played politics with the terrorist threat.

Yet, just because President Bush misjudged the nature of the threats facing the United States does not mean that serious threats to our national security do not exist. The terrorists are at war with us. The threat is from violent extremists who are a small minority of the world's 1.3 billion Muslims, but the threat is real. They distort Islam. They kill men, women, and children; Christians and Hindus, Jews and Muslims. They seek to create a repressive caliphate. To defeat this enemy, we must understand who we are fighting against and what we are fighting for.

It's time to break out of Washington's conventional thinking that has not kept pace with the unconventional threats we face. It's time to understand that we are facing a new kind of security challenge—and a new kind of enemy. Only by changing how we counter these threats and protect ourselves will we be able to make our nation safe and secure. As President, Barack Obama will:

Focus on Afghanistan and Pakistan.

The central front in the war on terror is not Iraq, and it never was. That's why ending the war in Iraq is essential if we want to finish the job against the terrorists who attacked us on 9/11—Al Qaeda and the Taliban in Afghanistan and Pakistan. Al Qaeda has reorganized to pre-9/11 strength, and the Taliban is resurgent. Osama bin Laden and Ayman al-Zawahiri are recording messages to their followers and plotting more terror. The Taliban controls parts of Afghanistan, and Al Qaeda has an expanding base of operations over the border in Pakistan. It is unacceptable that seven years after nearly three thousand Americans were killed on our soil, the terrorists who attacked us on 9/11 are still at large.

Barack Obama believes that our troops, working alongside our NATO allies, can defeat this threat. But as Admiral Mike Mullen, the Chairman of the Joint Chiefs of Staff, told the Senate this summer, we lack the troops to get the job done because of our commitment in Iraq. That's why, as President, Barack Obama will make the fight against Al Qaeda and the Taliban the top priority that it should be. To honor the memory of all those lost on 9/11, extinguish the threat posed by the central front of the war on terror, and to make America safe, this is a war that we must win.

Redeploy American Troops to Afghanistan.

Barack Obama will deploy at least an additional two brigades of American troops to Afghanistan to reinforce our counterterrorism operations and support NATO's efforts to fight the Taliban.

Strengthen NATO's Hand in Afghanistan.

Barack Obama will use an additional contribution of U.S. troops to press our NATO allies to do more. NATO currently has more than fifty thousand troops in Afghanistan. However, the force is short-staffed according to requirements laid down by NATO commanders. At the same time, some countries contributing forces are imposing restrictions on where their troops can operate, tying the hands of commanders on the ground. As President, Barack Obama will work with our European allies to end these burdensome restrictions and strengthen NATO as a fighting force.

Train and Equip the Afghan Army and Police.

In fall 2007, American Maj. Gen. Robert Durbin, who oversaw the training of Afghan security forces, said only 40 percent of the seventy-thousand-strong Afghan police force was properly equipped with weapons, communication equipment, and vehicles. The outgoing head of Canada's force in Afghanistan estimated it would take at least three years before Afghanistan's corruption-plagued police could stand on its own. Barack Obama will strengthen the training and equipping of the Afghan army and police and increase Afghan participation in U.S. and NATO missions, so that there is more of an Afghan face on security.

Increase Nonmilitary Aid to Afghanistan by $1 Billion.

Before the American invasion, Afghanistan was a failed state whose government did not provide for the security and needs of its people. It was the perfect environment for Al Qaeda to flourish. Today, Afghan security is undercut by lack of development, corruption, and drug trafficking. To prevent the country's backsliding into chaos, Barack Obama will increase U.S. nonmilitary aid to Afghanistan to $3 billion. This aid will fund reconstruction, police and army training, anticorruption efforts, promotion of rule of law and institutional development, and local projects, including efforts to impact the lives of ordinary Afghans and to give farmers alternatives to growing opium poppies. The aid will be part of a "more for more" approach—tied to better performance by the Afghan national government, including anticorruption initiatives and efforts to extend the rule of law across the country.

Demand More from the Pakistani Government.

As was made clear in a National Intelligence Estimate, Al Qaeda has successfully made the tribal areas of northern Pakistan a base from which to launch attacks into Afghanistan and beyond. We cannot tolerate such sanctuary for Al Qaeda, and as President, Barack Obama won't. He will condition U.S. military aid to Pakistan on their making progress to close down the training camps, evict foreign fighters, and prevent the Taliban from using Pakistan as a base to strike inside of Afghanistan. In addition, if the United States has actionable intelligence about high-value terrorist targets inside Pakistan, such as Osama bin Laden, and Pakistan will not act on it, an Obama Administration will.

Stand with the Pakistani People.

As the past year has shown, the choice in Pakistan is not between a military strongman and Islamist extremists. There is a vast moderate majority in that country, yearning for a better life and a better government. Barack Obama believes that by standing up for the aspirations of the Pakistani people, we can steady the stability of that nation. If not, we risk facing mounting popular opposition in a nuclear-armed nation at the nexus of terror and radical Islam. That's why an Obama Administration will triple nonmilitary aid to the Pakistani people and sustain it for the next decade. Moreover, we will ensure that the military assistance we do provide Pakistan is used to take the fight to the Taliban and Al Qaeda.

Work with Our Allies to Fight Terrorism.

Barack Obama will establish a Shared Security Partnership Program to invest $5 billion over three years to improve cooperation between U.S. and foreign intelligence and law enforcement agencies. This program will include information sharing, funding for training, operations, border security, anticorruption programs, technology, and the targeting of terrorist financing. And this effort will focus on helping our partners succeed without repressive tactics, because brutality breeds terror, it does not defeat it.

Launch a Public Diplomacy Effort.

Barack Obama will launch a coordinated, multi-agency program of public diplomacy. He will open "America Houses" in cities across the Arab world that would offer state-of-the-art English-language training programs, exposure to American culture and ideas, and offer free Internet access and moderated programs that promote direct exchange with Americans. An Obama Administration also will launch a new "America's Voice Corps" to rapidly recruit and train fluent speakers of local languages (Arabic, Bahasa, Farsi, Urdu, and Turkish) with public diplomacy skills, who can ensure our voice is heard in the mass media. Together these initia-

> *"We are at a defining moment in our history.*
> *We can choose the path of unending war*
> *and unilateral action, and sap our strength*
> *and standing . . . Or, we can meet fear and*
> *danger head-on with hope and strength,*
> *with common purpose as a united America,*
> *and with common cause with old allies*
> *and new partners."*
>
> —BARACK OBAMA, March 19, 2008, Fayetteville, North Carolina

tives will show the Muslim world the best America has to offer. Finally, as President, Barack Obama will lead this effort by example and by deed: during his first 100 days in office, President Obama will speak at a major Islamic forum to make clear that in the battle raging within Islam, the United States will stand with the moderate majority against the extremist minority and help them realize lives of opportunity and peace.

Restore America's Moral Authority.

The battle against Islamist terrorists is a battle to secure the United States of America and to win the hearts and minds of millions of Muslims who reject extremists' vision of the future. To win this contest, America must remain an example of the universal values and freedoms we hold dear. Understanding that America's standing, reputation, and authority in the world is critical to turning the tide against terrorism, Barack Obama will end the use of torture without exception and eliminate the practice of extreme rendition; close the Guantánamo Bay detention center; revise the PATRIOT Act so that it gives law enforcement the tools they need without jeopardizing the rights and ideals of all Americans; prevent illegal wiretapping; and restore the right of habeas corpus.

Prevent Bioterrorist Attacks.

Barack Obama will strengthen U.S. intelligence collection overseas to identify and interdict would-be bioterrorists before they strike, and will expand the U.S. government's bioforensics program for tracking the source of any biological weapon. An Obama Administration will work to ensure that countries meet their obligations under UN Security Council Resolution 1540 and the Biological and Toxin Weapons Convention to prevent terrorists and other states from developing and acquiring biological weapons.

Build Our Ability to Respond to a Bioterrorist Attack.

Biological weapons attacks could lead to large-scale epidemics that sicken and kill thousands and cause great disruption and economic loss. It's imperative that we prepare for the worst-case scenario. An Obama Administration will support increased research and development to improve our sensor technologies to detect attacks at the earliest possible stage, and will ensure that decision-makers have the information and communication tools they need to manage disease outbreaks by linking health care providers, hospitals, and public health agencies. It also will work to make it easier for hospitals and the wider medical community to work together to deal with sudden surges of patients and to make sure that they have the resources to diagnose and treat them.

Harden Our Cyber Infrastructure.

Information networks and computers play a vital role in every facet of our lives and are critical to our nation's economy, civil infrastructure, security, and military power. These networks, however, and the data that travels upon them, are under constant and increasing attack from foreign nations, terrorist organizations, and organized crime groups who are seeking to do damage to our nation, our companies, and our citizens. For the past eight years, the Bush Administration has dragged its feet in the face of this growing and new threat. An Obama Administration will provide federal leadership in strengthening our cyber security. It will work with industry and academia to develop and deploy a new generation of secure hardware and software for our nation's critical cyber infrastructure; protect the information technology infrastructure that keeps our vital systems—such as the electrical grid—running; and develop the systems necessary to protect our nation's trade secrets and our research and development.

Strengthen Homeland Security.

The first responsibility of any President is to protect the American people. Yet, seven years after the 9/11 attacks, our country is still unprepared to prevent and respond to a major terrorist attack or other catastrophe. We deserve better. That's why as President, Barack Obama will take every step to make our homeland more secure. An Obama Administration will:

- Allocate homeland security dollars according to risk, not as a form of general revenue sharing.
- Institute a regular review of our homeland security at least every four years to make sure we are prepared.
- Secure our chemical plants by setting a clear set of federal regulations that all plants must follow, including improving barriers, containment, mitigation, and safety training, and, where possible, using safer technology, such as less toxic chemicals.
- Strengthen the security and inspection capabilities of our ports so we know what is entering our nation.
- Support police, firefighters, and emergency medical professionals by rolling back the Bush funding cuts that have affected first responders and by increasing federal resources and logistic support to local emergency planning efforts.
- Make sure our first responders have interoperable communications systems and the equipment and training they need.
- Improve the sharing of information and intelligence among all levels of government.

Rebuild a Strong Twenty-first-Century Military

Ending the war in Iraq will be the beginning, but not the end, of addressing our defense challenges. We are now facing a whole new set of twenty-first-century security challenges, including terrorist networks with global reach, failing states that can provide them safe harbor, rogue nations—like Iran—that threaten their neighbors and support terrorists, and rising powers that could become adversaries.

Barack Obama honors the sacrifice of our troops and their families. He believes that it's critical that the Armed Forces are provided with the resources and leadership to remain the greatest fighting force the world has ever known. Yet right now, our military is being stretched to its limits. Our servicemen and -women are being strained by repeated and lengthy deployments, and by missions poorly conceived by the civilian leadership. Dwindling recruitment and retention rates threaten the strength of our all-volunteer force. The active-duty Army is short three thousand captains and majors, and 58 percent of recent West Point graduates are choosing to leave the force—nearly double the historic average. Our National Guard and Reserves have only half the equipment levels they need, hampering their ability to respond to crises, foreign and domestic.

America simply cannot afford more of the old approach to our national defense. Barack Obama will be a commander-in-chief with the right combination of judgment, vision, and leadership for the new century's challenges. As President, he will:

Increase the Size of Our Ground Forces.

A major stress on our troops comes from the insufficient size of our ground forces. Barack Obama supports plans to increase the size of the Army by 65,000 troops and the Marines by 27,000 troops. Increasing our end strength will help units retrain and re-equip properly between deployments and decrease the strain on military families. As President, Barack Obama will use the power of the bully pulpit to inspire a generation to serve their nation, especially in the Armed Forces.

Guarantee Our Ground Forces Have the Proper Training for New Challenges.

Barack Obama is a cosponsor of the Webb-Hagel plan to ensure that soldiers and Marines have sufficient training time before they are sent into battle. This is not the case at the moment, where American forces are being rushed to Iraq and Afghanistan, often with less individual and unit training than is required.

Fully Equip Our Troops for the Missions They Face.

We must listen to our ground commanders when they tell us what kinds of technology and skills they need to fight most effectively. We cannot repeat what happened in Iraq and fail to swiftly deploy up-armored vehicles in response to insurgent tactics. We must prioritize getting vitally needed equipment to our soldiers and Marines before lives are lost.

Reconfigure the Military to Handle New Threats.

As we rebuild our Armed Forces, we must meet the full spectrum of today's needs, not simply re-create the military of the Cold War era. An Obama Administration will reevaluate each major defense program in light of current needs, gaps in the field, and likely future threat scenarios in the post-9/11 world. As Commander-in-Chief, Barack Obama will build up our special operations forces, civil affairs, information operations, engineers, foreign area officers, and other units and capabilities that remain in chronic short supply. He will invest in foreign-language training, cultural awareness, and human intelligence and other needed counterinsurgency and stabilization skill sets. And he will create a specialized military advisors corps, which will enable us to better build up local allies' capacities to take on mutual threats.

Preserve America's Global Reach in the Air.

We must preserve our unparalleled airpower capabilities to deter and defeat any conventional competitors, swiftly respond to crises across the globe, and support our ground forces. To do that, we must have an Air Force that is best suited for current and future challenges. That's why Barack Obama believes we need greater investment in advanced technology ranging from unmanned aerial vehicles and electronic warfare capabilities to systems like the C-17 cargo and KC-X air-refueling aircraft.

Maintain American Naval Dominance.

The sea remains vital for global commerce and for rapidly positioning our forces in times of crisis to respond. To maintain the size of the fleet at an affordable cost, an Obama Administration will modernize the many capable ships that we now have and tilt the investment balance toward more capable, smaller combatants, while maintaining the Navy's ability to command the seas. It will increase investment in riverine craft and small coastal-patrol craft, and ensure the maximum interoperability between the Navy and the Coast

> *"Our country's greatest military asset is the men and women who wear the uniform of the United States."*
>
> —BARACK OBAMA, April 23, 2007, Chicago Council on Global Affairs

Guard. An Obama Administration also will work to maintain our shipbuilding design and industrial bases, and support increased research and development for naval forces.

Ensure Freedom of Space.

America's ability to use space as a location for its satellites and communications grid is critical to our national security and economy. Unfortunately, many nations are preparing to threaten space as a commons available to all nations. An Obama Administration will thoroughly assess possible threats to U.S. space assets and the best options, military and diplomatic, for countering them. It will then seek a code of conduct for space-faring nations, including a worldwide ban on weapons to interfere with satellites and a ban on testing anti-satellite weapons.

Support Our Armed Forces in the Field.

One of the best ways to support the brave men and women in our Armed Forces is to address the great imbalance in our executive branch capacity for dealing with twenty-first-century challenges that aren't of a purely military nature. That's why as President, Barack Obama will establish an expeditionary capability within non-Pentagon agencies (such as the Departments of State, Justice, and Treasury) to deploy personnel where they are needed. These civilians will be integrated with, and sometimes operate independently from, our military expeditionary capabilities, which will help move troops out of civilian roles and bring in the experts with the right expertise and skills. In addition, an Obama Administration will create an opportunity for skilled private citizens to help out by establishing a Civilian Assistance Corps (CAC) to provide each federal agency with a pool of volunteer experts willing to deploy in crises.

Improve Our Intelligence Efforts.

Gathering good intelligence and using it wisely is essential to maintaining our security. Barack Obama will improve the American intelligence apparatus by investing in its capacity to collect and analyze information, share information with other agencies, and carry out operations to disrupt terrorist operations and networks. To depoliticize intelligence gathering and analysis, Barack Obama supports making the Director of National Intelligence an official with a fixed term. To ensure that he gets critical assessments as President, Barack Obama will institutionalize the practice of developing competitive assessments of critical threats and strengthen our methodologies of analysis. And to develop our human capacity, Barack Obama will deploy and train more operatives and analysts with specialized knowledge of local languages and culture.

Restore the Readiness of the National Guard and Reserves.

The men and women of the National Guard and Reserves have performed valiantly, leaving their livelihoods—and risking their lives—to answer our nation's call. Yet, like their active-duty counterparts, the National Guard and Reserves have been stretched thin by the Administration's failure to provide adequate resources as well as its flawed foreign policy that has diverted the Guard and Reserves from critical homeland security missions and has subjected them to extended deployments. As President, Barack Obama will:

- Limit lengthy deployments to one year for every six years, restore the twenty-four-month limit on cumulative deployment time, and end the "Stop-Loss" program of forcing troops to stay in service beyond their expected commitments.
- Ensure the Guard and Reserves can meet their homeland security missions.
- Provide the Guard and Reserves with the resources and training they need.
- Fight discrimination against Guard and Reserves members in employment, and ensure that they are treated fairly when it comes to employment, health, and education benefits.

———

THOSE who serve in uniform are heroes, willing to give their lives for their fellow Americans. That's why it's so shameful when wounded warriors and veterans return home to poor care and a lack of needed services. As a grandson of a World War II veteran who went to college on the G.I. Bill and as a member of the Senate Committee on Veterans Affairs, Barack Obama has fought to improve care for troops recovering from injuries by sponsoring the Wounded Warrior bill, to combat homelessness among veterans, and to make the disability benefits process more equitable. When Barack Obama is President, building a twenty-first-century Department of Veterans Affairs (VA) to serve our veterans will be an equal priority to building a twenty-first-century military to fight our wars. His Secretary of Veterans Affairs will play a more active and central role than in Administrations past. As President, Barack Obama will:

Fully Fund Veterans' Medical Care.

The current Administration has consistently underinvested in the health care for our heroic veterans. In 2005, a multi-billion-dollar VA funding shortfall required Congress to step in and bail out the system. As President, Barack Obama will fully fund the VA so it has all the resources it needs to serve the veterans who need it, when they need it.

Improve Access to and Quality of Veterans' Medical Care.

Barack Obama believes that all veterans deserve quality care. He is committed to ending the unfair ban on health care enrollment of certain groups of veterans, including "Priority 8" veterans who often earn modest incomes. This ban has resulted in the VA turning away nearly one million veterans since 2003. As President, one of Barack Obama's first acts will be to sign an executive order reversing this ban. An Obama Administration also will expand the provision of specialty medical care and the number of centers focusing on Traumatic Brain Injury (TBI), post-traumatic stress disorder (PTSD), vision impairment, prosthetics, spinal cord injury, aging, women's health, and other specialized rehabilitative care. Finally, an Obama Administration will take on the massive backlog of hundreds of thousands of VA benefits claims. As President, Barack Obama will hire additional claims workers and spearhead an effort to develop an updated training and management model that will ensure that VA benefits decisions are rated fairly and consistently and stem from adequate training and accountability for each claims adjudicator.

Improve Mental Health Care.

Veterans returning from Iraq and Afghanistan are coming home with record levels of combat stress, but our military and VA medical systems are not adequately providing for them. As President, Barack Obama will improve mental health care at every stage of military service—recruitment, deployment, and reentry into civilian life. An Obama Administration will recruit more mental health care professionals, improve screening at the recruitment and post-deployment stages, and embed more mental health care professionals with troops.

Improve Transition Services for Returning Veterans.

As President, Barack Obama will ensure that the military and the VA coordinate to provide a truly seamless transition for service members from military to civilian life, including for reservists. To that end, an Obama Administration will extend the window for new veterans to enroll in the VA from two to five years, expand vet centers in rural areas, and make mental health services a priority.

Combat Homelessness Among Our Nation's Veterans.

On any given night, more than 200,000 veterans are homeless. However, the VA's homeless services reach only a quarter of this population. Barack Obama has been a leader in the fight to end homelessness among our nation's veterans. As a Senator, Barack Obama successfully passed legislation to expand services for homeless veterans. As President, Barack Obama will establish a national zero-tolerance policy for veterans falling into homelessness. He will improve existing services, expand proven homeless veteran housing vouchers to assist those already on the streets, and launch an innovative supportive services-housing program to prevent at-risk veterans and veteran families from falling into homelessness in the first place.

Lift the Onerous Burdens on Our Troops and Their Families.

Our military is built on families, and troops decide whether to reenlist based largely on how their families are faring. We must better support those families of whom we are asking so much. An Obama Administration will create a Military Families Advisory Board to help identify and develop actionable policies to ease the burden on spouses and families; support Family Readiness Groups; work to bring pay parity;

end the "back door draft" that allows an individual to be forced to remain on active duty after his or her enlistment has expired; and establish regularity in deployments so that active duty and reserves can plan their lives accordingly.

Expand Family Medical Leave to Cover Reserve Families Facing Deployment.

When a member of the Guard or Reserves is called away for active duty, their spouses have to make a tremendous transition and often struggle to balance work and family obligations. Barack Obama will expand Family Medical Leave to include Reserve families facing mobilization. This will allow workers whose spouses are called to active duty to get their affairs in order without losing their jobs.

Fight Veterans Employment Discrimination.

The current process of assisting reservists with employment discrimination complaints is ineffective. A discrimination complaint can take months to investigate and resolve, potentially leaving veterans vulnerable and stuck between jobs. Given the growing number of reservists demobilizing and seeking reemployment, we must make a long-term investment in improving the timeliness and quality of resolving these cases. As President, Barack Obama will invest additional resources into enforcement and investigation in order to crack down on employers who are not following the letter and spirit of the law.

Stop the Spread of Nuclear Weapons

For almost five decades, we worried about a nuclear stalemate with the Soviet Union. Now we need to worry about fifty tons of highly enriched uranium—some of it poorly secured—at civilian nuclear facilities in more than forty countries. We need to be concerned about the breakdown of a nonproliferation framework that was designed for the Cold War. And most of all, we need to make sure that a rogue state or nuclear scientist doesn't transfer the world's deadliest weapons to the world's most dangerous people. Make no mistake: terrorists and rogue nations won't think twice about killing hundreds of thousands in Tel Aviv, Cairo, London, or Chicago.

Over the past eight years, this threat has grown. It's a sad irony that the Bush Administration used concern over this threat to invade a country that didn't have a nuclear weapons program. And while we were preoccupied with Iraq, the technology to develop and deliver these weapons was spreading around the world.

We cannot wait any longer to protect the American people. In the Senate, Barack Obama made stopping the spread of nuclear weapons to terrorists and rogue nations a top priority. He worked with Republican Senator Richard Lugar to pass a law accelerating our pursuit of loose nuclear materials. As President, Barack Obama will continue this commitment. He has a comprehensive strategy for nuclear security that will reduce the danger of nuclear terrorism, prevent the spread of nuclear weapons capabilities, and strengthen the nuclear nonproliferation regime. He will:

Prevent Iran from Becoming a Nuclear Power.

Barack Obama is clear-eyed about the threat Iran poses to our interests and allies in the Middle East: Iran supports terrorists groups such as Hamas and Hezbollah; threatens the region's energy supplies; and has a president who not only denies the existence of the Holocaust, but also threatens to wipe Israel off the map. Our current policy toward Iran has not worked; over the past eight years, we have seen Iran strengthen its position, advance its nuclear program, and create 150 kilograms of low-enriched uranium in the first few months of this year alone. In addition, Tehran is threatening to trigger a nuclear arms race throughout the Middle East. Barack Obama believes that preventing Iran from developing nuclear weapons is a vital national security interest of the United States—and as such, no tool of statecraft or element of American power should be taken off the table in pursuit of this goal. This should start with aggressive, principled, and direct diplomacy—backed with strong sanctions. Barack Obama has been a leader in this effort, sponsoring legislation allowing and encouraging divestment from companies doing business in the Iranian energy sector. With a threat this grave, it's time that the United States takes an active role and leads the effort to prevent Iran from becoming a nuclear power.

Secure Nuclear Weapons Materials in Four Years.

To prevent terrorists from acquiring a nuclear bomb, Barack Obama will lead a global effort to secure all nuclear weapons materials at vulnerable sites within four years. An Obama Administration will increase funding by $1 billion a year to ensure that within four years, the essential ingredients of nuclear weapons are removed from all the world's most vulnerable sites and effective, lasting security measures are instituted for all remaining sites. As President, Barack Obama will work with Russia and other nations to make sure nuclear weapons and nuclear weapons materials in Russia and around the world are fully secured.

Phase Out Highly Enriched Uranium (HEU) from the Civil Sector.

HEU is not needed for the vast majority of civilian purposes, and most reactors using HEU should be converted to operate on low-enriched fuel that cannot be used in nuclear weapons or shut down so that terrorists cannot get their hands on it. With Barack Obama's leadership, the United States will lead the effort to remove HEU from vulnerable research reactor sites around the world, assist in the conversion process, give unneeded facilities incentives to shut down, enhance physical protection measures pending HEU removal, and blend down recovered civil HEU for use as power reactor fuel.

Strengthen Policing and Interdiction Efforts.

Barack Obama will institutionalize the Proliferation Security Initiative (PSI), a global initiative aimed at stopping shipments of weapons of mass destruction worldwide. He will expand the responsibilities of its members, not only in stopping illicit nuclear shipments, but also in eradicating nuclear black market networks.

Help Nations Prevent Theft, Diversion, or Spread of Nuclear Materials.

The global effort to stop nuclear proliferation is only as strong as its weakest link. UN Security Council Resolution 1540, which mandates that all nations implement effective domestic controls to prevent the proliferation of weapons of mass destruction, provides a potentially powerful tool for getting countries to institute effective nonproliferation controls. While the Bush Administration has failed to make effective use of this tool, the Obama Administration will reinvigorate this effort, helping all nations implement these controls. In addition, as President, Barack Obama will convene a summit in 2009 (and regularly thereafter) of the world's leading nations on how they can prevent nuclear terrorism.

Eliminate North Korea's Nuclear Weapons Programs.

North Korea is an example where direct, tough diplomacy that lays out clear choices to rogue regimes for good and bad behavior can lead to change. When the United States was engaged, the pace of Pyongyang's development of nuclear weapons was slowed; when we were not, it quickened. While there has been some promising progress, it's important that all of North Korea's claims are verified. If they are not, we should move quickly to reimpose sanctions that have been waived, and consider new restrictions going forward. As President, Barack Obama will work with diligence and determination with our friends and allies to end the threat of North Korea and to secure a lasting peace on the Korean peninsula.

Set the Goal of a World Without Nuclear Weapons.

Barack Obama will set a new direction in nuclear weapons policy and show the world that America believes in its existing commitment under the Nuclear Nonproliferation Treaty to work to ultimately eliminate all nuclear weapons. Barack Obama fully supports reaffirming this goal—as called for by George Shultz, Henry Kissinger, William Perry, and Sam Nunn—and the specific steps they propose to move us in that direction. He has made clear that America will not disarm unilaterally. Indeed, as long as states retain nuclear weapons, the United States will maintain a nuclear deterrent that is strong, safe, secure, and reliable. But as President, Barack Obama will not authorize the development of new nuclear weapons, and he will make the goal of eliminating nuclear weapons worldwide a central element of U.S. nuclear policy.

Strengthen the Nonproliferation Regime.

In an Obama Administration, the United States will lead the world in bolstering the international effort to prevent the spread of nuclear weapons and nuclear weapons material. To do this, Barack Obama will:

- Strengthen the International Atomic Energy Agency (IAEA) by making sure it gets the authority, information, people, and technology it needs to do its job and strengthen its ability to detect clandestine facilities and activities, including following through on a bipartisan effort with Senators Richard Durbin and Chuck Hagel

to provide $16 million in additional funding for the
IAEA.

- Lead a global effort to negotiate a verifiable treaty ending the production of fissile materials for weapons purposes.
- Establish a new international nuclear energy architecture
to meet growing demands for nuclear power without
contributing to the proliferation of nuclear materials
and fuel production facilities.
- Seek deep, verifiable reductions in all U.S. and Russian
nuclear weapons—whether deployed or nondeployed,
whether strategic or nonstrategic—and work with other
nuclear powers to reduce global stockpiles dramatically.
- Secure ratification of the Comprehensive Test Ban Treaty.

Renew Our Alliances to Meet New Global Challenges

In this new century, America faces threats that know no
national borders. They can arise from any corner of the
globe and spread anywhere, even to our shores: pandemic
disease, climate change, environmental degradation, failed
states, deep and persistent poverty, cyber attacks, international criminal networks, and terrorism. When a country in
Africa or Asia lacks the doctors, hospitals, and medicine to
inoculate its citizens from deadly infectious diseases, we too
are at risk. When children in the Middle East lack good
schools and have to turn to radical madrassas for education,

it's a setback in our battle against radical extremism. When a country has a government that refuses to listen to its people, provide for their material well-being, or can't control its own territory, that imperils our security. An Obama Administration will get out in front of these problems, helping those struggling around the world to achieve freedom from fear and freedom from want so that here at home we don't have to live in fear ourselves. In this new century, the security and well-being of each and every American is tied to the security and well-being of those who live beyond our borders.

To defuse these twenty-first-century threats, we must realize that while the United States is indispensable to tackling these challenges, we cannot do it alone. These transnational, global threats demand a global response, and the United States has the unique power of our values to inspire people around the world to our side. It is our responsibility—and in our interest—to lead these global efforts. As President, Barack Obama will:

End Our Long-Term Dependence on Foreign Oil.

The price of a barrel of oil is now one of the most dangerous weapons in the world. Tyrants from Caracas to Tehran use it to prop up their regimes, intimidate the international community, and hold us hostage to a market that is subject to their whims. The nearly $700 million a day we send to unstable or hostile nations funds our enemies in the war on terror, paying for everything from the madrassas that plant the seeds of terror in young minds to the bombs that go off in Baghdad and Kabul. It's time that the United States takes its fate into its own hands and out of those of dictators and tyrants. It's time to end our dependence on foreign oil. As President, Barack Obama will eliminate the need for the United States to import oil from the Middle East and Venezuela within ten years. An Obama Administration will double fuel economy standards within eighteen years—to save nearly a half trillion gallons of gasoline and 6 billion metric tons of greenhouse gases—while protecting the financial future of domestic automakers. And Barack Obama will expand tax credits to buy new ultra-efficient cars and increase the use of advanced biofuels.

Restructure Our Government to Meet Twenty-first-Century Challenges.

To meet these new challenges, more money is not the answer. We need to rethink and reinvent how we utilize and manage our government's resources. As President, Barack Obama will consolidate the many foreign assistance programs into a restructured, empowered, and streamlined USAID. He will ensure that the State Department has the authorities and resources it requires to lead U.S. government efforts to prevent and respond to conflict. He also will create Mobile Development Teams (MDTs) that bring together personnel from the military, the Pentagon, the State Department, and USAID, fully integrating U.S. government efforts in counterterror, state-building, and postconflict operations. And in time for the fiftieth anniversary of the Peace Corps in 2011, an Obama Administration will double its size from today's numbers.

> *"This must be the moment when we answer the call of history . . . We cannot afford four more years of a strategy that is out of balance and out of step with this defining moment."*
>
> —BARACK OBAMA, March 19, 2008, Fayetteville, North Carolina

Practice Tough Diplomacy.

In facing these twenty-first-century threats, Barack Obama believes we should use all the instruments of our power, including diplomacy, to ensure the safety and security of the United States. We should never fear meeting with our adversaries at a time and place of our choosing. It's the most effective way to take their measure and tell them the hard truths they don't want to hear. That's why throughout our history Presidents of both parties engaged some of our most significant adversaries: John Kennedy had a direct line to Nikita Khrushchev; Richard Nixon met with Mao Zedong; and Ronald Reagan negotiated arms agreements with Mikhail Gorbachev. As President, Barack Obama will use principled, tough diplomacy to let our adversaries know where we stand, push them to change their ways, and safeguard the American people.

Strengthen America's Partnerships and Alliances.

The United States is strongest when we act alongside strong partners. It's how we defeated Fascism and Communism in the twentieth century, and how we will overcome the security challenges of the twenty-first. As President, Barack Obama will:

- Rally our NATO allies to contribute more troops to collective security operations and to invest more in reconstruction and stabilization capabilities.
- Stand by and support our ally Israel. Barack Obama will bring to the White House an unshakable commitment to Israel's security. He will strengthen and deepen defense cooperation between our nations, isolate terrorist groups like Hamas and target their resources, stand up for Israel's right to defend itself from any threat, and make it clear that Israel's security is absolutely non-negotiable. To achieve lasting peace, Barack Obama will be an active partner in working to achieve a two-state solution, with a Jewish State of Israel living side-by-side in peace and security with a viable Palestinian state.
- Buttress our partnerships with Japan, South Korea, Australia, India, and other nations to forge a more effective framework in Asia that goes beyond bilateral agreements and occasional summits to create a stable and prosperous region.
- Engage China on common interests such as climate change while encouraging it to shift to a more open and free society and reform its trade policies.
- Vigorously engage South Africa and our friends in Southern Africa to put pressure on the vicious Mugabe regime in Zimbabwe.
- Lead the world in stopping the genocide in Darfur by imposing much tougher sanctions that target Sudan's

oil revenue, implementing and enforcing a no-fly zone, and supporting the deployment of a UN force to stop the killings.

- Reestablish American leadership in our hemisphere by following a strategy that advances democracy, security, and opportunity from the bottom up. This will include assisting the Colombian government in its struggle against the Revolutionary Armed Forces of Colombia (FARC) while pushing that country to respect labor and human rights; working with Mexico and Central America to crack down on transborder gang activity; and lifting up deeply poor countries like Haiti.

- Pursue a Cuba policy guided by one principle: liberty for the Cuban people. Empower the Cuban people to become less dependent on the Castro regime by giving Cuban-Americans unlimited rights to visit family on the island and to send them remittances. Pressure the Cuban regime to move toward democracy by maintaining the embargo and engaging in strong, principled, and direct diplomacy.

Rally the World to Stop Global Warming.

Carbon emissions released by countries across the globe are warming our planet, which leads to devastating weather patterns, terrible storms, drought, and famine. In fact, studies show that by 2050, famine could displace more than 250 million people worldwide. That means people competing for food and water in the next fifty years in the very places that have known horrific violence and instability in the last fifty: Africa, the Middle East, and South Asia. Climate change is a very real threat to our security, and we have precious little time to act. As President, Barack Obama will:

- Reduce America's carbon emissions 80 percent by 2050 through a market-based cap-and-trade system.
- Create the Global Energy Forum—a new forum of the largest greenhouse gas emitters that will lay the foundation for the next generation of climate protocols—and reengage in post-Kyoto international climate change negotiations.
- Invest $150 billion over the next decade to develop and deploy climate-friendly energy supplies, invest in energy-efficiency improvements, and address transition costs to new sources of energy.
- Develop alternative sources of energy, such as wind, solar, and biofuels.
- Transfer American technology to the developing world to fight climate change.
- Offer incentives to farmers and ranchers to maintain forests and manage them sustainably.

Double Foreign Assistance to $50 Billion.

Foreign assistance is a critical piece of our arsenal as we rise to these new challenges. As President, Barack Obama will double our annual investments in foreign assistance to $50 billion by 2012—into a range of programs from development to non-proliferation to counterterrorism—and ensure that these new resources are invested wisely with strong accountability measures and directed toward strategic goals.

Aim to Cut Extreme Poverty in Half by 2015.

Extreme poverty leads to states that are extremely unstable and could potentially spiral into armed conflict or provide havens to terrorists. Recognizing this, the United Nations has embraced the Millennium Development Goals, which aim to cut extreme poverty in half by 2015. However, the Bush Administration has tried to keep the UN from affirming these goals. In the Senate, Barack Obama cosponsored legislation to move the United States closer to support of these goals, and as President, he will make these goals America's. Barack Obama will also work to ensure that increases in U.S. assistance are matched by our partners in the G-8 so that developed countries truly live up to their stated commitments.

Fight Corruption.

Barack Obama believes that we must couple our assistance abroad with an insistent call for reform, transparency, and accountability. We also should demand that developing nations not waste American taxpayers' dollars, as well as put themselves on the path to the rule of law and root out corruption for their own citizens. As a starting point, an Obama Administration will add corruption to the annual human rights reports prepared by the State Department.

Eliminate the Global Education Deficit.

Education is the critical building block of social and economic development and is a key antidote to the hate peddled by extremists. Yet, today, across the developing world, one in five adults cannot read or write. Over 100 million children—and nearly 60 million girls—do not go to elementary school. The result is a staggering education deficit that traps people in poverty. Barack Obama will establish a Global Education Fund of at least $2 billion to help fill the financing gap for primary education, as recommended by the 9/11 Commission.

Lead the Effort to Combat HIV/AIDS, Tuberculosis, and Malaria.

There are an estimated 33 million people across the planet infected with HIV/AIDS, including more than 1 million people in the United States. Nearly 6,000 people die every day of AIDS. Barack Obama believes that we must do more to fight the global HIV/AIDS pandemic, as well as malaria and tuberculosis. The first priority should be implementing the recently signed President's Emergency Plan for AIDS Relief (PEPFAR) legislation that Barack Obama has long supported, ensuring that the best practices—not ideology—drive funding for HIV/AIDS programs. In that context, Barack Obama will commit $50 billion over five years to strengthen the existing program and expand it to new regions of the world, including Southeast Asia, India, and parts of Europe, where the HIV/AIDS burden is growing.

Establish Effective Global Health Infrastructure by 2020.

Developing nations need effective health care systems that can support a healthy workforce, sustain economic gains, and protect the citizenry from the threat of contagious diseases that know no borders. As President, Barack Obama will work with the private and philanthropic sectors to launch

Health Infrastructure 2020—a global effort to work with developing countries to invest in the full range of infrastructure needed to improve and protect both American and global health.

Provide Sustainable Debt Relief to Developing Countries.

The poorest countries in the world suffer under the weight of an enormous burden of external debt. Multilateral debt relief can be effective—thirty countries have seen their debt stocks reduced by almost 90 percent—but more relief is needed. An Obama Administration will be committed to living up to the promise to fully fund debt cancellation for Heavily Indebted Poor Countries (HIPC). His Administration also will dedicate itself to preventing a future in which poor countries face debt burdens again by pressing for reforms at the World Bank. Finally, as President, Barack Obama will lead a multilateral effort to examine how "loan sanctions" might be employed to create disincentives for private creditors to lend money to repressive, authoritarian regimes.

Achieve a World of Capable, Democratic States.

Over the past eight years, the long legacy of the United States standing up for democracy and human rights has been tarnished. Since our founding, the United States has been a "light unto the nations," and a beacon of hope to those yearning for liberty, equality, and democracy. Practically, democracies are our best trading partners, our most valuable allies, and the nations with which we share our deepest values. To achieve a world of capable, democratic states, Barack Obama will:

- Stand up for those struggling for human rights and speak out against dictators and tyrants.
- Help struggling democracies build strong legislatures and civil societies, instill the rule of law, and defend individuals' rights.
- Give direct support to opposition leaders pushing for democracy by significantly increasing funding for the National Endowment for Democracy.
- Create a Rapid Response Fund for societies in transition that will provide a catalyst to young democracies and post-conflict societies through foreign aid, debt relief, technical assistance, and investment packages.

PERFECTING
OUR UNION

EMBRACING AMERICA'S VALUES

"All my life, people have told me that my father changed their lives, that they got involved in public service or politics because he asked them to. I have never had a President who inspired me the way people tell me that my father inspired them. But I believe Barack Obama could be that President—a

President who reminds us that we all have something to contribute to this country that has given us so much."

—Caroline Kennedy

Vice Chair of New York City's Fund for Public Schools

"I've spent most of my life helping children rise up in some of this country's most devastated neighborhoods. I know persistent poverty and crime-ravaged neighborhoods and the look of despair in the eyes of kids who have lost hope. Barack Obama knows it, too. But we also know that hope is found in what works. I know he shares my commitment to changing the odds for our at-risk kids. And when he's President, I know we will."

—Geoffrey Canada

President and CEO of Harlem Children's Zone

Leading America at this critical moment in history requires more than policies and ideas. To meet our challenges, we must summon our common faith in American values—the sense of who we are as a people, the common beliefs that bind us together, the spirit of patriotism and service that bridges divisions of partisanship and ideology. How do we restore trust in a government that seems increasingly removed from its people and dominated by special interests? What does it mean to be a citizen and what does that title require of us? How do we resolve our differences at a time of increasing diversity? How do we honor our commitments to future generations?

E Pluribus Unum—"out of many, one"—are the words inscribed on the Great Seal of the United States. But we must make these words to live by with fundamental changes in government to restore the faith of the American people in our most important institutions. That means reforming Washington by reining in the power and influence of lobbyists who tilt policies toward narrow wealthy interests, often at the expense of the common good. It means opening up our government with greater transparency so average citizens can access the information they need to hold their leaders accountable. And it means inspiring and calling on all Americans to engage as citizens.

Our government has an important role to play in this work, and every aspect of it should be under review. We'll eliminate waste, streamline bureaucracy, and cut outmoded programs. An Obama Administration will open up the doors of democracy. It will put government data online, and use technology to shine a light on spending. It will invite the service and participation of American citizens, and cut through the red tape to make sure that every agency is meeting the highest standards. It will hold true to the obligations we have as stewards of our precious natural resources. And an Obama Administration will make sure that the doors of opportunity and community are open to all. We can't begin to tackle the challenges of the twenty-first century without the hard work, creativity, and patriotism of every American.

We also need leaders who recognize that government can do better, but it can't solve all our problems. Better education policies can improve our schools, but parents must provide the guidance our children need, turning off the TV and putting away the video games, attending parent-teacher conferences, helping with homework, and setting good, moral examples. Parents must teach our daughters to never allow images on television to tell them what they are worth. Parents must teach our sons to treat women with respect and to realize that what makes them men is not the ability to have a child but to have the courage to raise one. And we all must strive to be good neighbors and good citizens who are willing to volunteer in our communities—and to help our churches, synagogues, and community centers feed the hungry and care for the elderly. We all have to do our part to lift up this country.

In these times, the American people are not the problem; they are the answer. The values that we as a nation hold dear—faith and family, service and citizenship, community and country, responsibility and respect—are what make America strong and give meaning to our lives. And all of these will be part of Barack Obama's work in the White House.

Restore Trust in Government and Clean Up Washington

It is no coincidence that the disastrous policies of the past eight years have been accompanied by unprecedented access by lobbyists, the wealthy, and the well-connected as well as unprecedented governmental secrecy. In 2007, more than $2.8 billion was spent lobbying the federal government. The American people don't have that kind of money to spend on Washington, and they shouldn't have to. In our democracy, the price of access and influence should be nothing more than your voice and your vote. It's time to renew our politics in this country—to ensure that the hopes and concerns of average Americans speak louder in Washington than the hallway whispers of high-priced lobbyists.

As a State Senator, Barack Obama worked with Republicans and Democrats to pass the most sweeping ethics reform in Illinois history. In Washington, he challenged leaders of both parties to pass the toughest ethics legislation since Watergate. In this campaign, Barack Obama is leading by example. No registered lobbyists are employed by his presidential campaign. The campaign has not accepted a single dollar from Washington lobbyists, and Barack Obama has insisted that the Democratic National Committee do the same. As President, Barack Obama will restore the American people's trust in their government by limiting the influence of lobbyists and special interests; making government more open and transparent; and giving regular Americans unprecedented new tools to keep track of government officials— who they are meeting with, who is giving them money, and how they are spending taxpayer dollars. As President, Barack Obama will:

Close the Revolving Door Between Government and Lobbying Firms.

Public service should not be used as a stepping-stone to a career as a lobbyist. No political appointees in an Obama Administration will be permitted to work on regulations or contracts directly and substantially related to their prior employer for two years. And no political appointee will be able to lobby the executive branch after leaving government service during the remainder of an Obama Administration.

Ban Gifts to Executive Branch Employees.

Gifts from registered lobbyists—such as fancy dinners or

tickets to ball games—harm the political process because they give lobbyists an avenue for building and maintaining relationships that advance their agendas. As President, Barack Obama will issue an executive order banning registered lobbyists or lobbying firms from giving gifts in any amount or any form to executive branch employees.

Staff the Government Based on Talent, Not Political Loyalties.

Too often decisions in the executive branch, such as hiring and promotion, rely on ideology and political loyalty, with insufficient regard for competence and experience. Barack Obama will immediately issue an executive order asking all new hires at the agencies to sign a form affirming that no political appointee offered them the job solely on the basis of political affiliation or contribution. The executive order also will require that all employees engaged in and making hiring decisions certify that they will not take political affiliation into account as they make hiring decisions for career positions. As President, Barack Obama also will ban the use of public office to further partisan advantage in political elections. Finally, Barack Obama will require that political appointees possess relevant professional qualifications and experience related to the core mission of the agency for which they are nominated, thereby restoring integrity and competence to the executive branch.

Shine a Bright Light on Washington Lobbying.

When it comes to the corrupting influence of lobbyists on our politics, sunshine is truly the best disinfectant. This idea

> *"We need a President who sees government not as a tool to enrich friends and high-priced lobbyists, but as the defender of fairness and opportunity for every American. That's the kind of President I'll be."*
>
> —BARACK OBAMA, March 21, 2008, Tampa, Florida

drove Barack Obama to push Congress to pass the most sweeping lobbying-reform legislation since Watergate, and to work with Republican Senator Tom Coburn to pass "Google for Government," which created a powerful search engine for regular citizens to track federal grants, contracts, earmarks, and loans online. As a result, any individual can access a searchable database on the Internet to gather this information. As President, Barack Obama will build on these efforts to make sure that the public has specific, useful, and meaningful information about how lobbyists are trying to influence their elected officials. Barack Obama will:

- Create a centralized, online database of lobbying reports, tax earmarks, congressional ethics records, campaign finance filings, and information on how much federal contractors spend on lobbying.
- Expand the definition of "lobbying" to include lobbying for government contracts and presidential pardons.
- Establish an independent watchdog agency to investi-

gate congressional ethics violations. Right now, the fox guards the henhouse as members of Congress themselves conduct these investigations.

- Fight to disclose all contributions to organizations affiliated with the President or members of Congress.

Let Americans Track How Their Tax Dollars Are Spent.

Americans have a right to know how the government spends their tax dollars, but that information is usually hard to find and often not made available at all. As President, Barack Obama will change that by making this data easy to find and review. Barack Obama will:

- Give the public five days to review all nonemergency bills before they are signed into law, and not attach signing statements that undermine legislative intent.
- Hold politicians responsible for pork-barrel spending by disclosing the name of the legislator who asked for each earmark, asking for a written justification, and requiring seventy-two hours before they can be approved by the full Senate.
- End the abuse of no-bid contracts by requiring all contract orders over $25,000 to be competitively awarded unless the order falls within a specified exception and the contracting officer provides written justification.
- Clean up military contracting by establishing the reporting requirements, accounting, and accountability needed for good governance and cost savings, and ending no-bid contracting.

Bring Americans Back into Their Government.

Barack Obama will bring democracy and policymaking directly to the people by requiring his Cabinet officials to have periodic national broadband town hall meetings—twenty-first-century fireside chats—to discuss issues before their agencies. He will ensure that communications about regulatory policymaking between persons outside government and all White House staff are disclosed to the public. He will nullify President Bush's executive order hiding presidential records from the public and restore real meaning to the Freedom of Information Act. And as President, Barack Obama will require his appointees who lead the executive branch departments and rule-making agencies to conduct the significant business of the agency in public so that any citizen can see in person or watch on the Internet as the agencies debate and deliberate the issues that affect American society. Videos of meetings will be archived on the web, and the transcript will be available to the press and public.

Make Voluntary Citizen Service Universal

Throughout our history, Americans of every generation have stepped forward to serve their country: members of the military; suffragists and freedom riders; teachers and doctors; police officers, firefighters, and emergency response personnel. There is a lesson to be learned from their service: that while each of us is free to seek our own dreams, we have a duty to serve a common, higher purpose. Yet, in the wake of September 11, 2001, Americans did not receive a sustained call to service. The burden of sacrifice fell solely on those in uniform and their loved ones. It's time that every American is asked to serve, and given the opportunity to serve their community and country.

For Barack Obama, this is not just a policy plank, but the cause of his life. Whether it's helping communities deal with the hardships of steel mill closings or registering Americans to vote, Barack Obama has put public service first. He believes in the power of Americans to lift each other up and the transformative effect it has on individuals because he has lived it. As President, Barack Obama will ask Americans to serve, create new opportunities for Americans to serve, and direct that service to our most pressing national challenges. He will value and encourage military service across our society. His comprehensive national service plan will:

Expand AmeriCorps.

Since 1994, more than 500,000 people have served their communities through AmeriCorps. They have mentored inner-city children, weatherized homes, cared for the elderly, combated poverty, and helped communities prepare for and recover from natural disasters. Thousands of them have been on the front lines rebuilding New Orleans and the Gulf Coast after Katrina. AmeriCorps not only engages young people in full-time service that prepares them with experience and job skills, it also recruits experienced Americans for part-time service. Every year, AmeriCorps programs turn away tens of thousands of applicants because of limited funding. As President, Barack Obama will expand AmeriCorps from 75,000 slots today to 250,000, and he will focus this expansion on addressing the great challenges facing the nation. These additional slots will enable AmeriCorps to establish:

- **Classroom Corps** to recruit parents, grandparents, college students, or community members to mentor and provide one-on-one assistance to students, assist with classroom activities under the direction of teachers, and support after-school programs.
- **Health Corps** to improve public health information and outreach to areas with inadequate health systems, such as rural areas and inner cities.
- **Clean Energy Corps** to promote energy independence through efforts like cleaning up polluted land and water, planting trees, weatherization, renewable energy projects, and educational outreach.
- **Veterans Corps** to help keep America's sacred trust with its veterans by providing assistance at Department of Veterans Affairs facilities, nursing homes, homeless shelters, and elsewhere.
- **Homeland Security Corps** to help communities plan, prepare for, and respond to emergencies.

Engage Seniors in Service.

Seniors have a wide range of skills and knowledge to contribute to local and national public service efforts. New efforts are needed, particularly to tap the idealism and experience of the baby boomer generation—the largest and healthiest generation to enter retirement in history. Barack Obama will challenge experienced Americans to help meet the challenges in our communities and our country and will strengthen and

*"We need your service, right now, at this
moment—our moment—in history. . . .
I am going to ask you to play your part, ask
you to stand up, ask you to put your foot
firmly into the current of history."*

—BARACK OBAMA, June 2, 2008, Colorado Springs, Colorado

expand Senior Corps programs, AmeriCorps VISTA, and
Experience Corps. By supporting additional-income security,
including assistance with retirement and family-related costs,
and continuation of health care coverage, Barack Obama
will ensure that more seniors will be able to participate in
citizen service.

Double the Size of the Peace Corps.

Barack Obama will double the Peace Corps to 16,000 by its
fiftieth anniversary in 2011. He also will work with the leaders
of other countries to build an international network of overseas volunteers so that Peace Corps volunteers work side-by-
side with volunteers from other countries to address poverty,
combat diseases like HIV/AIDS and malaria, and reduce the
global education deficit.

Enlist Americans to Become Citizen-Diplomats.

Barack Obama will set up an America's Voice Initiative within
the State Department to rapidly recruit and train Americans
who are fluent speakers of local languages (Arabic, Bahasa,

Farsi, Urdu, and Turkish) in public diplomacy skills. These Americans will go overseas to ensure our voice is heard in the mass media and in our efforts on the ground. As President, Barack Obama also will create a Global Energy Corps composed of our scientists and engineers who will work with local partners overseas to help reduce global greenhouse gas emissions and promote low-carbon and affordable energy solutions in developing nations.

Expand Our All-Volunteer Military to Meet Current Needs.

A nation of 300 million strong should not be struggling to find enough qualified citizens to serve. Yet recruiting and retention problems have been swept under the rug by lowering standards and using the "Stop-Loss" program to keep our servicemen and -women in the force after their enlistment has expired. Even worse, the burdens of fixing these problems have been placed on the shoulders of young recruiting sergeants, instead of on leadership in Washington. At the same time, our security demands require us to expand our ground forces in both the Army and Marines. As President, Barack Obama will enable our all-volunteer military to meet these needs by making sure our troops have the training, support, and equipment they need and can receive high-quality education and health care benefits after they serve. Barack Obama also will use the bully pulpit of the presidency to encourage our young people to serve their country.

Create a "Craigslist" for Service.

Many Americans who want to serve are not aware of service opportunities that fit their interests or schedules, aren't sure how to distinguish among various opportunities, and don't know how to sign up. Technology can help. An Obama Administration will create a comprehensive, easily searchable web presence with information about service opportunities that will feature user ratings on volunteer experiences, ways to track hours of service, and social network features.

Expand Service-Learning in Our Nation's Public Schools.

Barack Obama's comprehensive plan to provide all Americans with a world-class education requires that school districts develop programs to engage students in service opportunities. Studies show that students who participate in service-learning programs do better in school, are more likely to graduate from high school and go to college, and are more likely to become active, engaged citizens. Schools that require service as part of the educational experience create improved learning environments and serve as resources for their communities. Barack Obama believes that middle and high school students should be expected to engage in community service for fifty hours annually during the school year or summer months. As President, he will develop national guidelines for service-learning and community service programs, and will give schools better tools both to develop successful programs and to document the experience of students at all levels.

Offer $4,000 Toward a College Education in Exchange for 100 Hours of Service.

Barack Obama will make college affordable for all Americans by creating a new American Opportunity Tax Credit that will ensure that the first $4,000 of a college education is completely free for most Americans, and will cover two-thirds the cost of tuition at the average public college or university. Recipients of this credit will be required to conduct 100 hours of public service a year, either during the school year or over the summer months. Barack Obama also believes we need to raise the service threshold in the Federal Work-Study program from 7 to 25 percent so that more students can afford to engage in public service. This will help more than 200,000 college students a year complete part-time public service while they are in school.

Connect Disadvantaged Youth to Service Opportunities.

In 2005, there were 1.7 million low-income sixteen- to twenty-four-year-olds out of school and unemployed who needed an opportunity to resume their education, find productive employment, and rebuild their lives. Barack Obama will establish a Green Job Corps to provide participants with service and job-training opportunities to improve energy conservation and efficiency of homes and buildings in their communities. In addition, an Obama Administration will expand the YouthBuild program that gives young people a chance to learn housing construction job skills and complete their high school education while they construct and rehabilitate affordable housing for low-income and homeless families.

Establish the Social Investment Fund Network.

Today, the nonprofit sector employs one in ten Americans, and 115 nonprofits are launched every day. In recent years, social entrepreneurs have been catalysts for much social inno-

vation in education, economic development, health, and the
environment. They do the bottom-up work that bureaucratic government cannot. To leverage private-sector funding
to improve local innovation and expand successful programs
to scale, Barack Obama will establish the Social Investment
Fund Network, a government-supported nonprofit corporation, similar to the Corporation for Public Broadcasting.
The fund will be results-oriented, respond to specific com-
munity-identified priorities, and focus on the long term.

Create a Social Entrepreneurship Agency for Nonprofits.

To unleash the potential power of nonprofit organizations and
help Americans create even more, Barack Obama will create a
social entrepreneurship agency, similar to the Small Business
Administration. This agency will improve the coordination of
programs that support nonprofits, foster nonprofit accountability, streamline the processes for obtaining federal grants
and contracts, and eliminate unnecessary requirements.

Partner with Communities of Faith

Faith can be a source of strength in our own lives. It has been
to Barack Obama since he first moved to Chicago as a young
man to work with a coalition of ministers to help the surrounding community, and it certainly is to many Americans.
But faith can also be something more: the foundation of a
new project of American renewal. Change comes not from
the top down, but from the ground up, and few are closer
to the people than our churches, synagogues, temples, and

> *"We know that faith and values can be a source of strength in our own lives. That's what it's been to me. And that's what it is to so many Americans. But it can also be something more. It can be the foundation of a new project of American renewal."*
>
> —BARACK OBAMA, July 1, 2008, Zanesville, Ohio

mosques. Washington needs to draw on their expertise and commitment—not as a replacement for government action, but as a complement to it. After all, many of our greatest challenges require the efforts of all sectors of our society. We need all hands on deck. As President, Barack Obama will:

Establish a New President's Council for Faith-Based and Neighborhood Partnerships.

This council will promote partnerships between government and faith-based and other nonprofit community groups to provide services to the needy and underserved. The council will train community and faith-based groups on how to apply for federal grants and comply with a web of federal laws and regulations, work closely with state and local governments to ensure that governors and mayors have the resources they need to support local organizations, and evaluate faith-based or secular community-serving nonprofits for effectiveness.

Train the Trainers.

Often it's hard for small congregations and organizations to learn what resources are available to them for their good works and how to access them. In an Obama Administration, the President's Council for Faith-Based and Neighborhood Partnerships will establish a Train the Trainers program to empower thousands of local faith-based social services organizations to train other local faith-based organizations on best practices, grant-making procedures, service delivery, and compliance with federal laws and regulations.

Set Guiding Principles for Federal Funding of Faith-Based Groups.

In an Obama Administration, the effort to work with faith-based and community groups will be guided by a core set of principles to ensure that such work is done in a way consistent with our values and constitutional principles. First, no program will be favored based on partisan or philosophical reasons. Second, faith-based organizations cannot use federal funds to proselytize or discriminate and must be held to the same standards of accountability as other federal grant recipients.

Strengthen Families

Barack Obama believes that of all the rocks upon which we build our lives, family is the most important. Fathers are critical to this foundation, but since 1960, the rate of American children without fathers in their lives has quadrupled, and more than 25 million children live without their biological fathers today. Children without fathers in their lives are five times more likely to live in poverty and are more likely to commit crime, drop out of school, and abuse drugs. Having been brought up by a single mother with a father whom he met only once after age two, Barack Obama knows first-hand how important it is that a child has as many loving family members as possible. Now the father of two girls, he understands the impact fathers can have on their children.

Barack Obama believes that if fathers are doing their part, then our government should meet them halfway by promoting responsible fatherhood and supporting families. We should be making it easier for fathers who make responsible choices and harder for those who avoid them. As President, Barack Obama will:

Sign the Responsible Fatherhood and Healthy Families Act.

Barack Obama believes that government should be making it easier for men to be involved in their children's lives, not harder. In the U.S. Senate, he introduced the Responsible Fatherhood and Healthy Families Act to remove government penalties on married families, crack down on men avoiding child support payments, ensure that child support payments go to families instead of state bureaucracies, and fund support services for fathers and their families, including domestic-violence prevention efforts. As President, Barack Obama will sign this bill into law.

Support Parents with Young Children.

The pioneering Nurse-Family Partnership provides visits to low-income expectant mothers and their families by trained registered nurses who use proven methods to help improve the mental and physical health of the family by providing counseling on substance abuse, creating and achieving personal goals, and effective methods of nurturing children. The results are improved women's prenatal health, a reduction in childhood injuries, fewer unintended subsequent pregnancies, increased father involvement and women's employment, reduced use of welfare and food stamps, and increased children's school readiness. Researchers at the RAND Corporation concluded that these initiatives produced more than five dollars in savings for every dollar invested and more than $30,000 in net savings for every high-risk family enrolled. As President, Barack Obama will increase federal funding through the SCHIP program to expand access to the Nurse-Family Partnership to all low-income first-time mothers, estimated to be about 570,000 per year.

Reward Parents Who Pay Their Child Support.

Government policy should make it easier for parents to raise their children, and should reward those who keep faith with their obligations to their kids. As President, Barack Obama will increase the number of working parents eligible for EITC benefits, increase the benefit available to parents who support their children through child support payments, increase the benefit for families with three or more children, and reduce the EITC marriage penalty, which hurts low-income families. Under the Obama plan, full-time workers making the minimum wage would get an EITC benefit up to $555, more than three times greater than the $175 benefit they get today. If the workers are responsibly supporting their children on child support, the Obama plan would give those workers a benefit of $1,110.

Make It Easier to Balance Work and Family.

Americans are finding it harder and harder to juggle the demands of work and of family. Not only are many parents struggling to find safe, enriching child care, but many are also now finding themselves caring for their aging and infirm parents. As a father of two small children and husband of a working woman, Barack Obama understands these demands deeply. As President, he will help families with their daily juggle. Specifically, an Obama Administration will expand the Family and Medical Leave Act to cover more employees and allow workers to take leave for elder care needs, for up to twenty-four hours each year to participate in their children's academic activities, and to address domestic-violence issues. It will encourage states to adopt paid family and medical leave. And he will double federal support for high-quality after-school activities, expand the Child and Dependent Care Tax Credit, and crack down on caregiver discrimination.

Advance Equal Opportunity for All Americans

Barack Obama understands that the greatness of this country—its victories in war, its enormous wealth, its scientific and cultural achievements—all result from the energy and imagination of the American people. If America is to meet the enormous challenges that lie ahead, we must ensure that all our citizens can fully participate in the American Dream and continue to contribute to our nation's greatness. As President, Barack Obama will fight discrimination, restore our commitment to equal justice, and expand opportunity for all Americans who are willing to work hard and contribute to our nation's future. Specifically, he will:

Close the Pay Gap for Women.

For every one dollar earned by a man, the average woman receives only 77 cents. According to the Institute for Women's Policy Research, closing the gender gap would lead to an economy-wide gain of $319 billion. This gap must be closed. As President, Barack Obama will:

- Provide a new "Making Work Pay" tax cut of up to $500 per person, or $1,000 per family, to 71 million working women, expand the Earned Income Tax Credit (EITC) to benefit at least 5 million working women, extend child care tax breaks to 7.5 million additional working women, and provide seven days of paid sick leave to 22 million working women who do not have this basic protection.
- Sign into law the Fair Pay Restoration Act, legislation that Barack Obama co-introduced to overturn last year's Supreme Court decision that made it harder for women to file pay-discrimination claims after they become victims of discriminatory compensation.
- Increase the minimum wage to $9.50 an hour and index it to inflation, a policy that will disproportionately benefit women.

- Give a hand up to women-owned small businesses by supporting their efforts to obtain capital, fighting discrimination in lending, and working to increase the percentage of women-owned businesses receiving federal contracts.

Strengthen Civil Rights Enforcement and Fight for a Fairer Justice System.

Over the past eight years, the Bush Administration has politicized the Department of Justice and has ground civil rights enforcement to a virtual halt. As President, Barack Obama will vigorously enforce our civil rights laws. He will fully fund and increase the staffing for the Equal Employment Opportunity Commission to reduce backlogs, reset the priorities of the Justice Department's Criminal Section and Civil Rights Division, reform sentencing disparities in the criminal justice system, and expand and fully enforce hate crimes statutes. An Obama Administration also will work to improve the quality of our nation's public defenders by creating loan-forgiveness programs for law students who enter this field.

End Racial Profiling.

As a State Senator, Barack Obama introduced and passed a law requiring the Illinois Department of Transportation to record the race, age, and gender of all drivers stopped for traffic violations so that bias could be detected and addressed. As a U.S. Senator, Barack Obama cosponsored federal legislation to ban racial profiling and require federal, state, and local law-enforcement agencies to take steps to eliminate the practice. As President, Barack Obama will continue his decades-long fight against racial profiling and sign legislation that will ban the practice by federal law-enforcement agencies, collect data on the extent of the problem, and provide federal funding to state and local police departments if they adopt policies to prohibit the practice.

Protect the Right to Vote.

Barack Obama has been a lifelong defender of voting rights. After law school, he led an effort that registered 150,000 new voters in Chicago. As a civil rights lawyer, he defended minority voters who challenged redistricting plans that diluted their vote. As a constitutional law lecturer, he taught classes on voting rights. And in the U.S. Senate, he has led the fight to reauthorize the Voting Rights Act, to oppose discriminatory photo-ID laws, and to improve our election machinery. As President, Barack Obama will sign into law the Deceptive Practices and Voter Intimidation Prevention Act, legislation he introduced to enable investigations into deceptive and fraudulent voting practices; establish significant, harsh penalties for those who have engaged in fraud; and provide voters who have been misinformed with accurate and full information so they can vote. In addition, he will fully fund the Help America Vote Act to make sure that we have modern, accurate voting systems across the country.

Support a Woman's Right to Choose.

Barack Obama understands that abortion is a divisive issue and respects those who disagree with him. However, he has been a consistent champion of reproductive choice and will make preserving women's rights under *Roe v. Wade* a priority as President. Barack Obama opposes late-term abortions, but believes that there must be exceptions for the life and health of the woman. He also supports preventing unintended pregnancies by increasing funding for family planning and comprehensive, age-appropriate sex education that teaches both abstinence and safe-sex methods. He will end insurance discrimination against contraception, improve awareness about emergency contraception, and provide compassionate assistance to rape victims.

Prevent Violence Against Women.

One in four women will experience domestic violence in her lifetime. Family violence accounted for 11 percent of all violence between 1998 and 2002. Barack Obama will promote partnerships that train staff in domestic-violence services, provide services to families affected by domestic violence, and develop best practices in prevention. He will strengthen domestic violence laws, and also fight gender violence abroad.

Empower Americans with Disabilities.

Barack Obama believes the United States should lead the world in empowering people with disabilities to take full advantage of their talents and become independent, integrated members of society. As President, Barack Obama will renew America's leadership by making the United States a signatory to the UN Convention on the Rights of Persons with Disabilities, restore the intent of the Americans with Disabilities Act, increase funding for the Individuals with Disabilities Education Act (IDEA), ensure that all states have comprehensive newborn-screening programs, increase federal support for Autism Spectrum Disorder initiatives to $1 billion per year, increase the employment rate of Americans with disabilities, and support independent and community-based living.

Prevent Discrimination Based on Sexual Orientation.

Barack Obama supports the Employment Non-Discrimination Act, supports full civil unions that give same-sex couples equal legal rights and privileges as married couples, and will expand adoption rights. As President, Barack Obama also will end discrimination in our armed forces based on sexual orientation by repealing the "Don't ask, don't tell" policy.

Enforce the Federal Government's Obligations to Native Americans.

Barack Obama supports the principle of tribal self-determination and will include tribal leadership in the important policy determinations that impact Indian Country. He supports sufficient funding for the Indian Health Service (IHS) and proper staffing and maintenance for IHS facilities, funding for Native language immersion and preservation programs, and more economic and infrastructure development.

Secure Our Borders and Reform a Broken Immigration System

Barack Obama believes it's time to put politics aside and embrace a comprehensive immigration policy that secures our border, enforces our laws, and reaffirms our heritage as a nation of immigrants. America has always been willing to give those in search of a better life the chance to come here, work hard, contribute to our nation, and realize their dreams of living in freedom and providing a brighter future for their children. Waves of immigrants over the years have contributed so much to our economy and our culture. America is also a nation of laws, and we must protect our borders. While most Americans agree on those core principles, immigration policy has been ineffective because it has been exploited by politicians to divide the nation rather than find real solutions. This has made the problem worse, made our borders less secure, and forced millions to live in the shadows of our society. As President, Barack Obama will:

Secure Our Borders.

Barack Obama wants to preserve the integrity of our borders. He supports additional personnel, infrastructure, and technology on the border and at our ports of entry. Barack Obama believes we need additional Customs and Border Protection agents equipped with better technology and real-time intelligence. He believes that physical fencing alone is not a solution to our immigration crisis, nor should it be the Secretary of Homeland Security's first recourse. As President, he will support physical fencing along the border where it makes sense as a matter of security and to act as a deterrent to unsafe, illegal entry. He will work with local officials on the border and in consultation with border communities to make sure that any additional fencing is not economically or environmentally destructive.

Crack Down on Employers That Hire Undocumented Immigrants.

Companies that hire undocumented workers are just as guilty of breaking the law as the people they hire. As a nation of laws, we need to hold everyone accountable. As President, Barack Obama will create a new employment eligibility verification system and make it mandatory and efficient for employers to verify that their employees are legally eligible to work in the United States.

Reform Our Immigration System.

Every year, a million people enter the country legally and another 500,000 to 800,000 people come without authorization or overstay their legal visas. The overwhelming majority of undocumented immigrants come to this country with the hope that hard work and sacrifice will secure a better life for their children, but to do so they break the law. Barack Obama believes we must require people to get right with the law. For those who have been working here and paying taxes, we should create a pathway to citizenship that puts the undocumented at the back of the line, behind those who came here legally. They should pay a fine, pay taxes, and learn English. Barack Obama also will promote citizenship for legal, documented immigrants by ensuring that application fees are reasonable and fair and making sure that all security background checks are accurate and timely. Finally, Barack Obama will improve our legal permanent-resident visa programs and temporary programs to attract some of the world's most talented people to America.

Honor Our Immigrant Troops.

About 65,000 foreign-born men and women serve in the U.S. armed forces, roughly 5 percent of the total active-duty force. Of those, more than 40,000 are not U.S. citizens. Barack Obama believes that legal immigrants who have fought for us overseas should have expedited procedures toward citizenship.

Safeguard the Environment for Future Generations

Just as it's critical that we stop the planet from warming, it's also important that we protect the air we breathe, the water we drink, and the soil in which we plant our crops. Doing so is the basis of a sacred trust we must safeguard for our children and grandchildren; their health and well-being depend on it. For too long, too many in Washington have sought to divide us over these issues, arguing that we could only either protect the environment or grow our economy. Barack Obama rejects that false choice. Throughout his career, he has worked to ensure that our nation's environmental laws and policies balance America's need for a healthy, sustainable environment with economic growth. In addition to his plan to reduce our dependence on foreign oil, address the challenge of climate change, and create five million new green jobs, Barack Obama will:

Fight for Clean Air.

During his service on the Senate Environment and Public Works Committee, Barack Obama helped stop President

Bush's attempt to undermine the Clean Air Act, which would have increased industrial emissions of mercury and sulfur. He has seen firsthand how the Bush Administration has harmed the health of our communities and the environment. As President, Barack Obama will restore the force of the Clean Air Act, fight for continued reductions in smog and soot, and continue his leadership in combating toxins that contribute to air pollution. He will listen to his scientific advisers on air quality standards, and will reverse the Bush Administration's attempts to chip away at our nation's clean air standards.

Clean Up Our Water.

Barack Obama will reinvigorate the Clean Water Act and drinking water standards that have been weakened under the Bush Administration and update them to address new threats. As President, he will help communities by restoring better federal financing for water and wastewater treatment infrastructure, and he will continue his leadership in protecting national treasures, like the Great Lakes and the Everglades, from threats such as industrial pollution, water diversion, and invasive species. Barack Obama also will establish policies to help high-growth regions with the challenges of managing their water supplies.

Restore Wetlands.

Barack Obama supports a broad range of traditional conservation programs, including the North American Wetlands Conservation Act and the Wetland Reserve Program in the Farm Bill. As President, he will work with local governments to develop the best strategies for protecting and expanding wetlands. He will also help the Gulf Coast restore the wetlands, marshes, and barrier islands that are critical to tamping down the force of hurricanes and serve as important fish and wildlife habitats.

Help the West Meet Its Water Demands.

The American West is facing a serious water crisis as we lack enough water to meet its fast-growing needs. Barack Obama believes the federal government has an important role to play in helping local communities conserve water. As President, he will support federal policies to encourage voluntary water banks, wastewater treatment, and other market-based conservation measures. He will also work to improve technology for water conservation and efficiency, and remove institutional barriers to increase cooperation and collaboration among federal, state, and private organizations.

Reduce Health Risks Caused by Mercury Pollution.

Nearly one in ten women of childbearing age have high levels of toxic mercury in their blood, and as many as 600,000 newborns are born every year at risk to mercury exposure. In the U.S. Senate, Barack Obama fought a Bush Administration rule that would have delayed meaningful reductions in power plant mercury emissions for another twenty years. In addition, to stop mercury emissions from overseas, Barack Obama successfully pressured the U.S. Department of Energy to stop its proposed sale of large quantities of mercury to companies overseas. As President, he will phase out the use of mercury in the manufacture of chlorine and will ban the export of elemental mercury.

Protect Children and Families from Lead Poisoning.

Lead is a neurotoxin that is especially harmful to the developing nervous systems of fetuses and young children. Following news reports that millions of Chinese-made toys were being recalled because of lead paint, Barack Obama pressured toy manufacturers and Bush Administration officials to do a better job of protecting American children. As President, Barack Obama will sign into law the Lead-Free Toys Act, which would require the Consumer Product Safety Commission to ban children's products containing more than trace amounts of lead. He also will further protect children from lead poisoning by requiring all non–home-based child care facilities, including Head Start programs and kindergartens, to be lead-safe within five years.

Make Polluters Pay.

Barack Obama demanded that the Environmental Protection Agency (EPA) report on what it is doing to reduce and control human exposure to hazardous contaminants at more than 100 heavily contaminated, toxic Superfund sites nationwide. As President, Barack Obama will reinvigorate the Superfund program by requiring polluters to pay for the cleanup of contaminated sites they created.

Fight for Environmental Justice.

Barack Obama will make environmental justice policies a priority within the EPA. As a U.S. Senator, Barack Obama has worked to ensure that low-income communities are represented in the EPA's long-term planning. As President, Barack Obama will work to strengthen the EPA Office of

Environmental Justice and expand the Environmental Justice Small Grants Program, which provides nonprofit organizations across the nation with valuable resources to address local environmental problems. He also will work to ensure that environmental health issues in the wake of man-made or terrorist disasters are promptly addressed by federal, state, and local officials. In addition, he will work to provide low-income communities the legal ability to challenge policies and processes that adversely affect the environmental health of low-income and minority communities.

Honor Sportsmen and Protect the Great Outdoors

Barack Obama did not grow up hunting and fishing, but he recognizes the great conservation legacy of America's hunters and anglers. Thanks to America's sportsmen, our nation has a longstanding tradition of access to lands on which to hunt, fish, camp, and hike. He will make sportsmen and their priorities a centerpiece of his land and water conservation agenda. As President, Barack Obama will:

Protect the Second Amendment.

Millions of hunters own and use guns each year. Millions more participate in a variety of shooting sports, such as sporting clays, skeet, target, and trap shooting. Barack Obama believes the Second Amendment creates an individual right, and he greatly respects the constitutional rights of Americans to bear arms. As President, he will protect the rights of hunters and other law-abiding Americans to purchase, own, transport, and use guns for the purposes of hunting and target sports. He also believes that this right is subject to reasonable and commonsense regulation that can help us keep guns off the streets and away from criminals and terrorists, such as closing the gun-show loophole and repealing the Tiahrt Amendment to give police officers the tools they need to solve gun crimes and fight the illegal arms trade.

Expand Access to Places to Hunt, Fish, Camp, and Hike.

American hunters and anglers are losing access to places to hunt and fish. As President, Barack Obama will make the conservation of private lands a priority and work to ensure access to our public lands for hunting, fishing, camping, and hiking. He will fight to increase funding for the Conservation Security Program and the major set-aside programs such as the Conservation Reserve Program, Wetlands Reserve Program, and Grasslands Reserve Program, so that rental rates can compete with rising commodity prices.

Preserve the Habitats That Sportsmen Enjoy.

Barack Obama is fully committed to protecting the habitat for the fish and wildlife that sportsmen enjoy. He is an advocate for preserving our wetlands and supports a broad range of national conservation programs, including the North American Wetlands Conservation Act, the Land and Water Conservation Fund, and the National Fish Habitat Plan. An Obama Administration will also put an unprecedented level of emphasis on the conservation of private lands. As President, Barack Obama will advance legislation that works with landowners to focus federal attention and increase resources for this effort, and will create additional incentives for private landowners to protect and restore wetlands, grasslands, forests, and other wildlife habitats. He will also implement a new energy policy that protects the most important fish and wildlife habitats, wildlife corridors, and other areas while ensuring responsible energy development on our public lands.

Conserve Our National Parks and Forests.

America's national parks and forests are treasures that belong not just to every American, but to Americans in generations to come. Yet for too long, our national parks and forests have been threatened by lax protection. As a U.S. Senator, Barack Obama fought efforts to drill in the Arctic National Wildlife Refuge, and supports the protection of roadless areas to keep over 58 million acres of national forests pristine. As President, Barack Obama will repair the damage done to our national parks by inadequate funding and emphasize the conservation of our national forests. To conserve pristine places abroad, Barack Obama would prohibit the importation of illegally harvested wood products. This would make foreign companies much less likely to engage in massive, illegal deforestation in other countries. Saving these endangered forests preserves a major source of carbon sequestration.

Fight Crime and Promote Public Safety

Whether they live in cities, suburbs, or small towns, too many Americans reside in communities where drugs, illegal guns, and gangs have wreaked havoc and undermined law and order. Barack Obama believes that keeping our communities safe is an indispensable part of empowering all Americans to succeed, no matter where they live. His plan will support local law enforcement and reduce violence and other crimes. As President, Barack Obama will:

Put 50,000 More Police Officers on the Beat.

The Bush Administration has consistently cut funding for Community Oriented Policing Services (COPS), a key funding source for putting more police officers on the beat. As President, Barack Obama will fully fund the COPS program to put 50,000 police officers on the beat over the next six years, and hire 1,000 new FBI agents over that same time period. He also will support efforts to encourage young people to enter the law-enforcement profession to ensure that our local police departments are not understaffed because of a dearth of qualified applicants.

Crack Down on Drugs and Gangs.

The Bush Administration has consistently proposed to cut or eliminate funding for the Byrne Justice Assistance Grant (Byrne/JAG) program, which funds antidrug and antigang task forces across the country. Byrne/JAG also funds drug prevention and treatment programs that are critical to reducing U.S. demand for drugs. Since 2000, this program has been cut more than 83 percent, threatening hundreds of antidrug and antigang task forces—many that took years to create and develop. In the U.S. Senate, Barack Obama has been a leader in the fight to maintain funding for these vital programs. As President, he will restore funding to this important effort.

Take Back Neighborhoods from Drugs.

Barack Obama will support the expansion of the innovative and effective Weed-and-Seed initiative, where law-enforcement personnel work to "weed out" violent offenders and drug users while public agencies and private organizations plant the "seeds" of vital services in the community. Together, these groups work to reduce crime, prevent future criminal acts and future criminals, intervene in problem areas, and extend treatment to those who need it.

End the Dangerous Cycle of Youth Violence.

As a resident of and former community organizer on the South Side of Chicago, Barack Obama has witnessed first-hand the destructive nature of youth violence and gang activity on our children and entire communities. As President, Barack Obama will support innovative, public health–based local programs, such as the CeaseFire program in Chicago, that have been proven to work in breaking the cycle of youth violence. Barack Obama will also double the funding for federal after-school programs and invest in twenty Promise Neighborhoods across the country to ensure that urban youth have safe and meaningful opportunities to keep them out of trouble after school.

Keep Drugs Off of America's Streets.

Successfully keeping drugs off of America's streets requires a comprehensive approach that transcends the boundaries between local, state, and federal law enforcement. Furthermore, it requires the close cooperation of international allies like Mexico and Canada. As President, Barack Obama will work with his Attorney General and Secretary of Homeland Security to create a comprehensive strategy on regional crime that addresses the United States's contribution to the problem. Barack Obama's "southbound" strategy will target the trafficking of guns, money, and stolen vehicles that go virtually unchecked from the United States south into Mexico and beyond. Critical to this strategy will be ensuring an adequate number of U.S. federal agents to police trafficking on our borders. Barack Obama will pair this "southbound" strategy with our existing "northbound" strategy that is aimed at drug and human traffickers, as well as illegal immigration. Barack Obama also has been a leader in fighting the methamphetamine epidemic. As President, he will restrict the importation of precursor chemicals used to make meth, and work with countries around the world to take down international criminal drug rings. Moreover, he will establish federal drug courts, mirroring the success these courts have had at the state level.

Stop Repeat Offenders.

One of the toughest problems in keeping our neighborhoods safe is preventing criminals from becoming repeat offenders and falling into a life of crime. Up to two-thirds of the 650,000 prisoners released every year are rearrested within three years. That's why it's so important to break this cycle and put offenders on the path to responsible citizenship. As President, Barack Obama will create a prison-to-work incentive program, modeled on the successful Welfare-to-Work Partnership, to create ties with employers and third-party agencies who provide training and support services to ex-offenders and to improve ex-offender employment and job-retention rates. He also will work to reform correctional systems to break down barriers for ex-offenders to find employment.

Recruit More Neighborhood Prosecutors.

Neighborhood prosecution programs have given residents of at-risk municipalities a direct line to the criminal justice system. Prosecutors take an active role in the community by attending town hall meetings, establishing field offices, and working closely with law enforcement and residents to respond to criminal activity. An Obama Administration will support the recruitment of more prosecutors to this program.

Guarantee the Rights of Victims.

As an Illinois State Senator, Barack Obama understood that the impact of a crime on a victim should be a principal factor in handing down punishment and passed a bill to grant a victim or his or her spouse, parent, guardian or other immediate family the right to make a statement in court during sentencing. Barack Obama will continue the work he has done throughout his public life to give crime victims a greater say in sentencing.

Register and Restrict Sex Offenders.

As the father of two young daughters, Barack Obama is keenly aware of the dangers our children face. Barack Obama helped create a national sex offender database through his cosponsorship of Dru's Law. As President, he will support the KIDS Act, which requires sex offenders to provide their Internet identifiers (e-mail addresses, instant messaging tags, etc.) for use in the National Sex Offender Public Registry.

Protect Our Children Online.

Just as in the real world, there are some dark corners of the Internet where material unsuitable for children can be found and where criminals lurk. An Obama Administration will give parents the tools and information they need to control what their children see on television and the Internet. Barack Obama will encourage improvements to the existing voluntary rating system, exploiting new technologies like tagging and filtering, so that parents can better understand what content their children will see and have the tools to respond. He also will ensure that parents have the option of receiving parental-controls software that not only blocks objectionable Internet content but also prevents children from revealing personal information through their home computer. Finally, as President, Barack Obama will institute tough penalties, increase enforcement resources and forensic tools, and collaboration between law enforcement and the private sector to identify and prosecute people who abuse the Internet to try to exploit children.

CONCLUSION

YES WE CAN

The stakes of this election are high—higher than perhaps they've ever been.

Our economy is reeling. Our health care costs are higher than ever. A college education is becoming harder to afford just when it's needed most. Our nation is at war and faces new and different threats to our national security. Our climate is warming.

Our country is on the wrong track, and everyone reading this book knows it. You know it when you kiss a loved one good-bye as he or she is deployed overseas for the second or third time, see your neighbor's home foreclosed on, look at the balance of your retirement account, or fill up your gas tank. The dream that so many generations of Americans fought for—that one's children will do better than they did—feels as if it's slowly slipping away. Most of all, too many have lost faith that our leaders can, or will, do anything about it.

But at this moment, in this election, we have the opportunity—and the obligation—to chart a new course for this country.

Barack Obama believes that ordinary citizens—Democrats, Republicans, and independents—are ready to unite in the cause of renewing America's promise. He believes it's time to look beyond partisanship and division and move toward a common ground and real solutions. It's time for us to reaffirm our shared values of faith and family, hard work and sacrifice, fairness and equal opportunity for all—and create a brighter future for our nation.

There is little doubt that the American people can compete—and succeed—in the twenty-first century. Our quintessentially American mix of optimism, dynamism, and determination can help us meet this moment. But we will also need leadership with the judgment to make tough decisions, with the foresight to see around the next bend in history, and with the fortitude to stand up to entrenched, outdated thinking and chart a new path. We need a leader who can unite us around the principles that we share and rally us to a common purpose.

As President of the United States, Barack Obama will provide that leadership. He will jump-start our economy, give a hand up to families struggling to make ends meet, and ensure that hard work is rewarded with a decent living. And looking to the generations to come, he will prepare our country to lead the industries of tomorrow, by turning the United States into a leader in the green economy and investing in science, technology, and infrastructure.

Barack Obama will provide new leadership for a changing world—ending the war in Iraq, finishing the fight against Al Qaeda and the Taliban, and leading the world to tackle the new threats of this century. He will unite our country around our shared values, stop the lobbyists from dominating our government, and return the power in Washington back to the American people.

Millions of Americans—from all parts of this country, from all backgrounds, and from all walks of life—support Barack Obama because they too believe that America is on the wrong track and because they too believe that whenever faced with adversity, Americans don't despair. We roll up our sleeves. We call our neighbors, family, and friends to lend a hand. We work at our problems until we get it right. We never give up.

And guiding us is a belief in the power we have if we all work together, a fidelity to the history we share, and an indomitable spirit that always believes: yes we can.

PART 2
THE CALL

DECLARATION OF
CANDIDACY

February 10, 2007 | *Springfield, Illinois*

L ET ME BEGIN by saying thanks to all of you who've traveled, from far and wide, to brave the cold today.

We all made this journey for a reason. It's humbling, but in my heart I know you didn't come here just for me; you came here because you believe in what this country can be. In the face of war, you believe there can be peace. In the face of despair, you believe there can be hope. In the face of a politics that's shut you out, that's told you to settle, that's divided us for too long, you believe we can be one people, reaching for what's possible, building that more perfect union.

That's the journey we're on today. But let me tell you how I came to be here. As most of you know, I am not a native of this great state. I moved to Illinois over two decades ago. I was a young man then, just a year out of college; I knew no one in Chicago, was without money or family connections. But a group of churches had offered me a job as a community organizer for $13,000 a year. And I accepted the job, sight unseen, motivated then by a single, simple, powerful idea—that I might play a small part in building a better America.

My work took me to some of Chicago's poorest neighborhoods. I joined with pastors and laypeople to deal with communities that had been ravaged by plant closings. I saw that the problems people faced weren't simply local in nature—that the decision to close a steel mill was made by distant executives; that the lack of textbooks and computers in schools could be traced to the skewed priorities of politicians a thousand miles away; and that when a child turns to violence, there's a hole in his heart no government alone can fill.

It was in these neighborhoods that I received the best education I ever had, and where I learned the true meaning of my Christian faith.

After three years of this work, I went to law school, because I wanted to understand how the law should work for those in need. I became a civil rights lawyer and taught constitutional law, and after a time, I came to understand that our cherished rights of liberty and equality depend on the active participation of an awakened electorate. It was with these ideas in mind that I arrived in this capital city as a State Senator.

It was here, in Springfield, where I saw all that is America converge—farmers and teachers, businessmen and laborers, all of them with a story to tell, all of them seeking a seat at the table, all of them clamoring to be heard. I made lasting friendships here—friends that I see in the audience today.

It was here we learned to disagree without being disagreeable—that it's possible to compromise so long as you know those principles that can never be compromised; and that so long as we're willing to listen to each other, we can assume the best in people instead of the worst.

That's why we were able to reform a death penalty system that was broken. That's why we were able to give health insurance to children in need. That's why we made the tax system more fair and just for working families, and that's why we passed ethics reforms that the cynics said could never, ever be passed.

It was here, in Springfield, where north, south, east, and west come together that I was reminded of the essential decency of the American people—where I came to believe that through this decency, we can build a more hopeful America.

And that is why, in the shadow of the Old State Capitol, where Lincoln once called on a divided house to stand together, where common hopes and common dreams still live, I stand before you today to announce my candidacy for President of the United States.

I recognize there is a certain presumptuousness—a certain audacity—to this announcement. I know I haven't spent a lot of time learning the ways of Washington. But I've been there long enough to know that the ways of Washington must change.

The genius of our founders is that they designed a system of government that can be changed. And we should take heart, because we've changed this country before. In the face of tyranny, a band of patriots brought an empire to its knees. In the face of secession, we unified a nation and set the captives free. In the face of Depression, we put people back to work and lifted millions out of poverty. We welcomed immigrants to our shores, we opened railroads to the west, we landed a man on the moon, and we heard a King's call to let justice roll down like water, and righteousness like a mighty stream.

Each and every time, a new generation has risen up and done what's needed to be done. Today we are called once more—and it is time for our generation to answer that call.

For that is our unyielding faith—that in the face of impossible odds, people who love their country can change it.

That's what Abraham Lincoln understood. He had his doubts. He had his defeats. He had his setbacks. But through his will and his words, he moved a nation and helped free a people. It is because of the millions who rallied to his cause that we are no longer divided, North and South, slave and free. It is because men and women of every race, from every walk of life, continued to march for freedom long after Lincoln was laid to rest, that today we have the chance to face the challenges of this millennium together, as one people— as Americans.

All of us know what those challenges are today—a war with no end, a dependence on oil that threatens our future, schools where too many children aren't learning, and families struggling paycheck to paycheck despite working as hard as they can. We know the challenges. We've heard them. We've talked about them for years.

What's stopped us from meeting these challenges is not the absence of sound policies and sensible plans. What's stopped us is the failure of leadership, the smallness of our politics—the ease with which we're distracted by the petty and trivial, our chronic avoidance of tough decisions, our preference for scoring cheap political points instead of rolling up our sleeves and building a working consensus to tackle big problems.

For the last six years we've been told that our mounting debts don't matter, we've been told that the anxiety Americans feel about rising health care costs and stagnant wages are an illusion, we've been told that climate change is a hoax, and that tough talk and an ill-conceived war can replace diplomacy, and strategy, and foresight. And when all else fails, when Katrina happens, or the death toll in Iraq mounts, we've been told that our crises are somebody else's fault. We're distracted from our real failures and told to blame the other party, or gay people, or immigrants.

And as people have looked away in disillusionment and frustration, we know what's filled the void. The cynics, and the lobbyists, and the special interests who've turned our government into a game only they can afford to play. They write the checks and you get stuck with the bills, they get the access while you get to write a letter, they think they own this government, but we're here today to take it back. The time for that politics is over. It's time to turn the page.

We've made some progress already. I was proud to help lead the fight in Congress that led to the most sweeping ethics reform since Watergate.

But Washington has a long way to go. And it won't be easy. That's why we'll have to set priorities. We'll have to make hard choices. And although government will play a crucial role in bringing about the changes we need, more money and programs alone will not get us where we need to go. Each of us, in our own lives, will have to accept responsibility—for instilling an ethic of achievement in our children, for adapting to a more competitive economy, for strengthening our communities, and sharing some measure of sacrifice. So let us begin. Let us begin this hard work together. Let us transform this nation.

Let us be the generation that reshapes our economy to compete in the digital age. Let's set high standards for our schools and give them the resources they need to succeed. Let's recruit a new army of teachers and give them better pay and more support in exchange for more accountability. Let's make college more affordable, and let's invest in scientific research, and let's lay down broadband lines through the heart of inner cities and rural towns all across America.

And as our economy changes, let's be the generation that ensures our nation's workers are sharing in our prosperity. Let's protect the hard-earned benefits their companies have promised. Let's make it possible for hardworking Americans to save for retirement. And let's allow our unions and their organizers to lift up this country's middle class again.

Let's be the generation that ends poverty in America. Every single person willing to work should be able to get job training that leads to a job, and earn a living wage that can pay the bills, and afford child care so their kids have a safe place to go when they work. Let's do this.

Let's be the generation that finally tackles our health care crisis. We can control costs by focusing on prevention, by providing better treatment to the chronically ill, and using technology to cut the bureaucracy. Let's be the generation that says right here, right now, that we will have universal health care in America by the end of the next President's first term. Let's be the generation that finally frees America from the tyranny of oil. We can harness homegrown, alternative fuels like ethanol and spur the production of more fuel-efficient cars. We can set up a system for capping greenhouse gases. We can turn this crisis of global warming into a moment of opportunity for innovation, and job creation, and an incentive for businesses that will serve as a model for the world. Let's be the generation that makes future generations proud of what we did here.

Most of all, let's be the generation that never forgets what happened on that September day and confront the terrorists with everything we've got. Politics doesn't have to divide us on this anymore—we can work together to keep our country safe. I've worked with Republican Senator Dick Lugar to pass a law that will secure and destroy some of the world's deadliest, unguarded weapons. We can work together to track terrorists down with a stronger military, we can tighten the net around their finances, and we can improve our intelligence capabilities. But let us also understand that ultimate victory against our enemies will come only by rebuilding our alliances and exporting those ideals that bring hope and opportunity to millions around the globe.

But all of this cannot come to pass until we bring an end to this war in Iraq. Most of you know I opposed this war from the start. I thought it was a tragic mistake. Today we grieve for the families who have lost loved ones, the hearts that have been broken, and the young lives that could have been. America, it's time to start bringing our troops home. It's time to admit that no amount of American lives can resolve the political disagreement that lies at the heart of someone else's civil war. That's why I have a plan that will bring our combat troops home by March of 2008. Letting the Iraqis know that we will not be there forever is our last, best hope to pressure the Sunni and Shia to come to the table and find peace.

Finally, there is one other thing that is not too late to get right about this war, and that is the homecoming of the men and women—our veterans—who have sacrificed the most. Let us honor their valor by providing the care they need and rebuilding the military they love. Let us be the generation that begins this work.

I know there are those who don't believe we can do all these things. I understand the skepticism. After all, every four years, candidates from both parties make similar promises, and I expect this year will be no different. All of us running for President will travel around the country offering ten-point plans and making grand speeches; all of us will trumpet those qualities we believe make us uniquely qualified to lead the country. But too many times, after the election is over, and the confetti is swept away, all those promises fade from memory, and the lobbyists and the special interests move in, and people turn away, disappointed as before, left to struggle on their own.

That is why this campaign can't only be about me. It must be about us—it must be about what we can do together. This campaign must be the occasion, the vehicle, of your hopes, and your dreams. It will take your time, your energy, and your advice—to push us forward when we're doing right, and to let us know when we're not. This campaign has to be about reclaiming the meaning of citizenship, restoring our sense of common purpose, and realizing that few obstacles can withstand the power of millions of voices calling for change.

By ourselves, this change will not happen. Divided, we are bound to fail.

But the life of a tall, gangly, self-made Springfield lawyer tells us that a different future is possible.

He tells us that there is power in words.

He tells us that there is power in conviction.

That beneath all the differences of race and region, faith and station, we are one people.

He tells us that there is power in hope.

As Lincoln organized the forces arrayed against slavery, he was heard to say: "Of strange, discordant, and even hostile elements, we gathered from the four winds, and formed and fought to battle through."

That is our purpose here today.

That's why I'm in this race.

Not just to hold an office, but to gather with you to transform a nation.

I want to win that next battle—for justice and opportunity.

I want to win that next battle—for better schools, and better jobs, and health care for all.

I want us to take up the unfinished business of perfecting our union, and building a better America.

And if you will join me in this improbable quest, if you feel destiny calling, and see, as I see, a future of endless possibility stretching before us; if you sense, as I sense, that the time is now to shake off our slumber, and slough off our fear, and make good on the debt we owe past and future generations, then I'm ready to take up the cause, and march with you, and work with you. Together, starting today, let us finish the work that needs to be done, and usher in a new birth of freedom on this Earth.

IOWA CAUCUS NIGHT

January 3, 2008 | *Des Moines, Iowa*

T HANK YOU, IOWA.

You know, they said this day would never come.

They said our sights were set too high.

They said this country was too divided; too disillusioned to ever come together around a common purpose.

But on this January night—at this defining moment in history—you have done what the cynics said we couldn't do. You have done what the state of New Hampshire can do in five days. You have done what America can do in this new year, 2008. In lines that stretched around schools and churches; in small towns and big cities; you came together as Democrats, Republicans, and independents to stand up and say that we are one nation; we are one people; and our time for change has come.

You said the time has come to move beyond the bitterness and pettiness and anger that's consumed Washington; to end the political strategy that's been all about division and instead make it about addition—to build a coalition for change that stretches through Red states and Blue states. Because that's how we'll win in November, and that's how we'll finally meet the challenges that we face as a nation.

We are choosing hope over fear. We're choosing unity over division and sending a powerful message that change is coming to America.

You said the time has come to tell the lobbyists who think their money and their influence speak louder than our voices that they don't own this government, we do; and we are here to take it back.

The time has come for a President who will be honest about the choices and the challenges we face; who will listen to you and learn from you even when we disagree; who won't just tell you what you want to hear, but what you need to know. And in New Hampshire, if you give me the same chance that Iowa did tonight, I will be that President for America.

Thank you.

I'll be a President who finally makes health care affordable and available to every single American the same way I expanded health care in Illinois—by—by bringing Democrats and Republicans together to get the job done.

I'll be a President who ends the tax breaks for companies that ship our jobs overseas and put a middle-class tax cut into the pockets of the working Americans who deserve it.

I'll be a President who harnesses the ingenuity of farmers and scientists and entrepreneurs to free this nation from the tyranny of oil once and for all.

And I'll be a President who ends this war in Iraq and finally brings our troops home; who restores our moral standing; who understands that 9/11 is not a way to scare up votes, but a challenge that should unite America and the world against the common threats of the twenty-first century; common threats of terrorism and nuclear weapons; climate change and poverty; genocide and disease.

Tonight, we are one step closer to that vision of America because of what you did here in Iowa. And so I'd especially like to thank the organizers and the precinct captains; the volunteers and the staff who made this all possible.

And while I'm at it, on thank-yous, I think it makes sense for me to thank the love of my life, the rock of the Obama family, the closer on the campaign trail—give it up for Michelle Obama.

I know you didn't do this for me. You did this . . . you did this because you believed so deeply in the most American of ideas—that in the face of impossible odds, people who love this country can change it.

I know this—I know this because while I may be standing here tonight, I'll never forget that my journey began on the streets of Chicago doing what so many of you have done for this campaign and all the campaigns here in Iowa—organizing, and working, and fighting to make people's lives just a little bit better.

I know how hard it is. It comes with little sleep, little pay, and a lot of sacrifice. There are days of disappointment, but sometimes, just sometimes, there are nights like this—a night . . . a night that, years from now, when we've made the changes we believe in; when more families can afford to see a doctor; when our children—when Malia and Sasha and your children—inherit a planet that's a little cleaner and safer, when the world sees America differently, and America sees itself as a nation less divided and more united; you'll be able to look back with pride and say that this was the moment when it all began.

This was the moment when the improbable beat what Washington always said was inevitable.

This was the moment when we tore down barriers that have divided us for too long—when we rallied people of all parties and ages to a common cause; when we finally gave Americans who'd never participated in politics a reason to stand up and to do so.

This was the moment when we finally beat back the politics of fear, and doubt, and cynicism; the politics where we tear each other down instead of lifting this country up. This was the moment.

Years from now, you'll look back and you'll say that this was the moment—this was the place—where America remembered what it means to hope.

For many months, we've been teased, even derided, for talking about hope.

But we always knew that hope is not blind optimism. It's not ignoring the enormity of the task ahead or the roadblocks that stand in our path. It's not sitting on the sidelines or shirking from a fight. Hope is that thing inside us that insists, despite all evidence to the contrary, that something better awaits us if we have the courage to reach for it, and to work for it, and to fight for it.

Hope is what I saw in the eyes of the young woman in Cedar Rapids who works the night shift after a full day of college and still can't afford health care for a sister who's ill; a young woman who still believes that this country will give her the chance to live out her dreams.

Hope is what I heard in the voice of the New Hampshire woman who told me that she hasn't been able to breathe since her nephew left for Iraq; who still goes to bed each night praying for his safe return.

Hope is what led a band of colonists to rise up against an empire; what led the greatest of generations to free a continent and heal a nation; what led young women and young men to sit at lunch counters and brave fire hoses and march through Selma and Montgomery for freedom's cause.

Hope . . . hope . . . is what led me here today—with a father from Kenya; a mother from Kansas; and a story that could only happen in the United States of America. Hope is the bedrock of this nation; the belief that our destiny will not be written for us, but by us; by all those men and women who are not content to settle for the world as it is; who have the courage to remake the world as it should be.

That is what we started here in Iowa, and that is the message we can now carry to New Hampshire and beyond; the same message we had when we were up and when we were down; the one that can change this country brick by brick, block by block, calloused hand by calloused hand—that, together, ordinary people can do extraordinary things; because we are not a collection of Red states and Blue states, we are the United States of America; and at this moment, in this election, we are ready to believe again. Thank you, Iowa.

NEW HAMPSHIRE
PRIMARY NIGHT

January 8, 2008 | *Nashua, New Hampshire*

I WANT TO congratulate Senator Clinton on a hard-fought victory here in New Hampshire.

A few weeks ago, no one imagined that we'd have accomplished what we did here tonight. For most of this campaign, we were far behind, and we always knew our climb would be steep.

But in record numbers, you came out and spoke up for change. And with your voices and your votes, you made it clear that at this moment—in this election—there is something happening in America.

There is something happening when men and women in Des Moines and Davenport, in Lebanon and Concord, come out in the snows of January to wait in lines that stretch block after block because they believe in what this country can be.

There is something happening when Americans who are young in age and in spirit—who have never before participated in politics—turn out in numbers we've never seen because they know in their hearts that this time must be different.

There is something happening when people vote not just for the party they belong to but the hopes they hold in common—that whether we are rich or poor, black or white, Latino or Asian; whether we hail from Iowa or New Hampshire, Nevada, or South Carolina, we are ready to take this country in a fundamentally new direction. That is what's happening in America right now. Change is what's happening in America.

You can be the new majority who can lead this nation out of a long political darkness—Democrats, independents, and Republicans who are tired of the division and distraction that have clouded Washington; who know that we can disagree without being disagreeable; who understand that if we mobilize our voices to challenge the money and influence that's stood in our way and challenge ourselves to reach for something better, there's no problem we can't solve—no destiny we cannot fulfill.

Our new American majority can end the outrage of unaffordable, unavailable health care in our time. We can bring doctors and patients, workers and businesses, Democrats and Republicans together; and we can tell the drug and insurance industry that while they'll get a seat at the table, they don't get to buy every chair. Not this time. Not now.

Our new majority can end the tax breaks for corporations that ship our jobs overseas and put a middle-class tax cut into the pockets of the working Americans who deserve it.

We can stop sending our children to schools with corridors of shame and start putting them on a pathway to success. We can stop talking about how great teachers are and start rewarding them for their greatness. We can do this with our new majority.

We can harness the ingenuity of farmers and scientists, citizens and entrepreneurs, to free this nation from the tyranny of oil and save our planet from a point of no return.

And when I am President, we will end this war in Iraq and bring our troops home; we will finish the job against Al Qaeda in Afghanistan; we will care for our veterans; we will restore our moral standing in the world; and we will never use 9/11 as a way to scare up votes, because it is not a tactic to win an election, it is a challenge that should unite America and the world against the common threats of the twenty-first century: terrorism and nuclear weapons; climate change and poverty; genocide and disease.

All of the candidates in this race share these goals. All have good ideas. And all are patriots who serve this country honorably.

But the reason our campaign has always been different is because it's not just about what I will do as President, it's also about what you, the people who love this country, can do to change it.

That's why tonight belongs to you. It belongs to the organizers and the volunteers and the staff who believed in our improbable journey and rallied so many others to join.

We know the battle ahead will be long, but always remember that no matter what obstacles stand in our way, nothing can withstand the power of millions of voices calling for change.

We have been told we cannot do this by a chorus of

cynics who will only grow louder and more dissonant in the weeks to come. We've been asked to pause for a reality check. We've been warned against offering the people of this nation false hope.

But in the unlikely story that is America, there has never been anything false about hope. For when we have faced down impossible odds; when we've been told that we're not ready, or that we shouldn't try, or that we can't, generations of Americans have responded with a simple creed that sums up the spirit of a people.

Yes we can.

It was a creed written into the founding documents that declared the destiny of a nation.

Yes we can.

It was whispered by slaves and abolitionists as they blazed a trail toward freedom through the darkest of nights.

Yes we can.

It was sung by immigrants as they struck out from distant shores and pioneers who pushed westward against an unforgiving wilderness.

Yes we can.

It was the call of workers who organized; women who reached for the ballot; a President who chose the moon as our new frontier; and a King who took us to the mountaintop and pointed the way to the Promised Land.

Yes we can to justice and equality. Yes we can to opportunity and prosperity. Yes we can heal this nation. Yes we can repair this world. Yes we can.

And so tomorrow, as we take this campaign south and west, as we learn that the struggles of the textile worker in Spartanburg are not so different than the plight of the dishwasher in Las Vegas; that the hopes of the little girl who goes to a crumbling school in Dillon are the same as the dreams of the boy who learns on the streets of LA; we will remember that there is something happening in America: that we are not as divided as our politics suggests; that we are one people; we are one nation; and together, we will begin the next great chapter in America's story with three words that will ring from coast to coast; from sea to shining sea. Yes. We. Can.

A MORE PERFECT UNION

March 18, 2008 | Philadelphia, Pennsylvania

"WE THE PEOPLE, in order to form a more perfect union."

Two hundred and twenty-one years ago, in a hall that still stands across the street, a group of men gathered and, with these simple words, launched America's improbable experiment in democracy. Farmers and scholars; statesmen and patriots, who had traveled across an ocean to escape tyranny and persecution, finally made real their declaration of independence at a Philadelphia convention that lasted through the spring of 1787.

The document they produced was eventually signed but ultimately unfinished. It was stained by this nation's original sin of slavery, a question that divided the colonies and brought the convention to a stalemate until the founders chose to allow the slave trade to continue for at least twenty more years, and to leave any final resolution to future generations.

Of course, the answer to the slavery question was already embedded within our Constitution—a Constitution that had at its very core the ideal of equal citizenship under the law; a Constitution that promised its people liberty, and justice, and a union that could be and should be perfected over time.

And yet words on a parchment would not be enough to deliver slaves from bondage, or provide men and women of every color and creed their full rights and obligations as citizens of the United States. What would be needed were Americans in successive generations who were willing to do their part—through protests and struggle, on the streets and in the courts, through a civil war and civil disobedience and always at great risk—to narrow that gap between the promise of our ideals and the reality of their time.

This was one of the tasks we set forth at the beginning of this campaign—to continue the long march of those who came before us, a march for a more just, more equal, more free, more caring, and more prosperous America. I chose to run for the presidency at this moment in history because I believe deeply that we cannot solve the challenges of our time unless we solve them together—unless we perfect our union by understanding that we may have different stories, but we hold common hopes; that we may not look the same and we may not have come from the same place, but we all want to move in the same direction—toward a better future for our children and our grandchildren.

This belief comes from my unyielding faith in the decency and generosity of the American people. But it also comes from my own American story.

I am the son of a black man from Kenya and a white woman from Kansas. I was raised with the help of a white grandfather who survived a Depression to serve in Patton's army during World War II and a white grandmother who worked on a bomber assembly line at Fort Leavenworth while he was overseas. I've gone to some of the best schools in America and lived in one of the world's poorest nations. I am married to a black American who carries within her the blood of slaves and slave owners—an inheritance we pass on to our two precious daughters. I have brothers, sisters, nieces, nephews, uncles, and cousins of every race and every hue scattered across three continents, and for as long as I live, I will never forget that in no other country on Earth is my story even possible.

It's a story that hasn't made me the most conventional candidate. But it is a story that has seared into my genetic makeup the idea that this nation is more than the sum of its parts—that out of many, we are truly one.

Throughout the first year of this campaign, against all predictions to the contrary, we saw how hungry the American people were for this message of unity. Despite the temptation to view my candidacy through a purely racial lens, we won commanding victories in states with some of the whitest populations in the country. In South Carolina, where the Confederate flag still flies, we built a powerful coalition of African Americans and white Americans.

This is not to say that race has not been an issue in the campaign. At various stages in the campaign, some commentators have deemed me either "too black" or "not black enough." We saw racial tensions bubble to the surface during the week before the South Carolina primary. The press has scoured every exit poll for the latest evidence of racial polarization, not just in terms of white and black, but black and brown as well.

And yet, it has only been in the last couple of weeks that the discussion of race in this campaign has taken a particularly divisive turn.

On one end of the spectrum, we've heard the implication that my candidacy is somehow an exercise in affirmative action; that it's based solely on the desire of wide-eyed liberals to purchase racial reconciliation on the cheap. On the other end, we've heard my former pastor, Reverend Jeremiah Wright, use incendiary language to express views that have the potential not only to widen the racial divide, but views that denigrate both the greatness and the goodness of our nation, that rightly offend white and black alike.

I have already condemned, in unequivocal terms, the statements of Reverend Wright that have caused such controversy. For some, nagging questions remain. Did I know him to be an occasionally fierce critic of American domestic and foreign policy? Of course. Did I ever hear him make remarks that could be considered controversial while I sat in church? Yes. Did I strongly disagree with many of his political views? Absolutely—just as I'm sure many of you have heard remarks from your pastors, priests, or rabbis with which you strongly disagreed.

But the remarks that have caused this recent firestorm weren't simply controversial. They weren't simply a religious leader's effort to speak out against perceived injustice. Instead, they expressed a profoundly distorted view of this country—a view that sees white racism as endemic, and that elevates what is wrong with America above all that we know is right with America; a view that sees the conflicts in the Middle East as rooted primarily in the actions of stalwart allies like Israel, instead of emanating from the perverse and hateful ideologies of radical Islam.

As such, Reverend Wright's comments were not only wrong but divisive, divisive at a time when we need unity; racially charged at a time when we need to come together to solve a set of monumental problems—two wars, a terrorist threat, a failing economy, a chronic health care crisis, and potentially devastating climate change; problems that are neither black or white or Latino or Asian, but rather problems that confront us all.

Given my background, my politics, and my professed values and ideals, there will no doubt be those for whom my statements of condemnation are not enough. Why associate myself with Reverend Wright in the first place, they may ask? Why not join another church? And I confess that if all that I knew of Reverend Wright were the snippets of those sermons that have run in an endless loop on the television and YouTube, or if Trinity United Church of Christ conformed to the caricatures being peddled by some commentators, there is no doubt that I would react in much the same way.

But the truth is, that isn't all that I know of the man. The man I met more than twenty years ago is a man who helped introduce me to my Christian faith, a man who spoke to me about our obligations to love one another, to care for the sick and lift up the poor. He is a man who served his country as a U.S. Marine, who has studied and lectured at some of the finest universities and seminaries in the country, and who for over thirty years led a church that serves the community by doing God's work here on Earth—by housing the homeless, ministering to the needy, providing day care services and scholarships and prison ministries, and reaching out to those suffering from HIV/AIDS.

In my first book, *Dreams from My Father,* I described the experience of my first service at Trinity:

> People began to shout, to rise from their seats and clap and cry out, a forceful wind carrying the reverend's voice up into the rafters. And in that single note—hope!—I heard something else; at the foot of that cross, inside the thousands of churches across the city, I imagined the stories of ordinary black people merging with the stories of David and Goliath, Moses and Pharaoh, the Christians in the lion's den, Ezekiel's field of dry bones. Those stories—of survival, and freedom, and hope—became our story, my story; the blood that had spilled was our blood, the tears our tears; until this black church, on this bright day, seemed once more a vessel carrying the story of a people into future generations and into a larger world. Our trials and triumphs became at once unique and universal, black and more than black; in chronicling our journey, the stories and songs gave us a means to reclaim memories that we didn't need to feel shame about—memories that all people might study and cherish—and with which we could start to rebuild.

That has been my experience at Trinity. Like other predominantly black churches across the country, Trinity embodies the black community in its entirety—the doctor and the welfare mom, the model student and the former gangbanger. Like other black churches, Trinity's services are full of raucous laughter and sometimes bawdy humor. They are full of dancing, clapping, screaming, and shouting that may seem jarring to the untrained ear. The church contains in full the kindness and cruelty, the fierce intelligence and the shocking ignorance, the struggles and successes, the love and, yes, the bitterness and bias that make up the black experience in America.

And this helps explain, perhaps, my relationship with Reverend Wright. As imperfect as he may be, he has been like family to me. He strengthened my faith, officiated my wedding, and baptized my children. Not once in my conversations with him have I heard him talk about any ethnic group in derogatory terms, or treat whites with whom he interacted with anything but courtesy and respect. He contains within him the contradictions—the good and the bad—of the community that he has served diligently for so many years.

I can no more disown him than I can disown the black community. I can no more disown him than I can my white grandmother—a woman who helped raise me, a woman who sacrificed again and again for me, a woman who loves me as much as she loves anything in this world, but a woman who once confessed her fear of black men who passed by her on the street, and who on more than one occasion has uttered racial or ethnic stereotypes that made me cringe.

These people are a part of me. And they are a part of America, this country that I love.

Some will see this as an attempt to justify or excuse

comments that are simply inexcusable. I can assure you it is not. I suppose the politically safe thing would be to move on from this episode and just hope that it fades into the woodwork. We can dismiss Reverend Wright as a crank or a demagogue, just as some have dismissed Geraldine Ferraro, in the aftermath of her recent statements, as harboring some deep-seated racial bias.

But race is an issue that I believe this nation cannot afford to ignore right now. We would be making the same mistake that Reverend Wright made in his offending sermons about America—to simplify and stereotype and amplify the negative to the point that it distorts reality.

The fact is that the comments that have been made and the issues that have surfaced over the last few weeks reflect the complexities of race in this country that we've never really worked through—a part of our union that we have yet to perfect. And if we walk away now, if we simply retreat into our respective corners, we will never be able to come together and solve challenges like health care, or education, or the need to find good jobs for every American.

Understanding this reality requires a reminder of how we arrived at this point. As William Faulkner once wrote, "The past isn't dead and buried. In fact, it isn't even past." We do not need to recite here the history of racial injustice in this country. But we do need to remind ourselves that so many of the disparities that exist in the African-American community today can be directly traced to inequalities passed on from an earlier generation that suffered under the brutal legacy of slavery and Jim Crow.

Segregated schools were, and are, inferior schools; we still haven't fixed them, fifty years after *Brown v. Board of Education,* and the inferior education they provided, then and now, helps explain the pervasive achievement gap between today's black and white students.

Legalized discrimination—where blacks were prevented, often through violence, from owning property, or loans were not granted to African-American business owners, or black home owners could not access FHA mortgages, or blacks were excluded from unions, or the police force, or fire departments—meant that black families could not amass any meaningful wealth to bequeath to future generations. That history helps explain the wealth and income gap between black and white, and the concentrated pockets of poverty that persist in so many of today's urban and rural communities.

A lack of economic opportunity among black men, and the shame and frustration that came from not being able to provide for one's family, contributed to the erosion of black families—a problem that welfare policies for many years may have worsened. And the lack of basic services in so many urban black neighborhoods—parks for kids to play in, police walking the beat, regular garbage pick up, and building code enforcement—all helped create a cycle of violence, blight, and neglect that continues to haunt us.

This is the reality in which Reverend Wright and other African Americans of his generation grew up. They came of age in the late fifties and early sixties, a time when segregation was still the law of the land and opportunity was systematically constricted. What's remarkable is not how many failed in the face of discrimination, but rather how many

men and women overcame the odds, how many were able
to make a way out of no way for those like me who would
come after them.

But for all those who scratched and clawed their way to
get a piece of the American Dream, there were many who
didn't make it—those who were ultimately defeated, in one
way or another, by discrimination. That legacy of defeat was
passed on to future generations—those young men and increasingly young women who we see standing on street corners or languishing in our prisons, without hope or prospects
for the future. Even for those blacks who did make it, questions of race, and racism, continue to define their worldview
in fundamental ways. For the men and women of Reverend
Wright's generation, the memories of humiliation and doubt
and fear have not gone away; nor has the anger and the bitterness of those years. That anger may not get expressed in
public, in front of white coworkers or white friends. But it
does find voice in the barbershop or around the kitchen
table. At times, that anger is exploited by politicians, to gin
up votes along racial lines, or to make up for a politician's
own failings.

And occasionally it finds voice in the church on Sunday
morning, in the pulpit and in the pews. The fact that so many
people are surprised to hear that anger in some of Reverend
Wright's sermons simply reminds us of the old truism that
the most segregated hour in American life occurs on Sunday
morning. That anger is not always productive; indeed, all
too often it distracts attention from solving real problems;
it keeps us from squarely facing our own complicity in our
condition, and prevents the African-American community

from forging the alliances it needs to bring about real change. But the anger is real; it is powerful; and to simply wish it away, to condemn it without understanding its roots, only serves to widen the chasm of misunderstanding that exists between the races.

In fact, a similar anger exists within segments of the white community. Most working- and middle-class white Americans don't feel that they have been particularly privileged by their race. Their experience is the immigrant experience—as far as they're concerned, no one's handed them anything, they've built it from scratch. They've worked hard all their lives, many times only to see their jobs shipped overseas or their pension dumped after a lifetime of labor. They are anxious about their futures, and feel their dreams slipping away; in an era of stagnant wages and global competition, opportunity comes to be seen as a zero sum game, in which your dreams come at my expense. So when they are told to bus their children to a school across town, when they hear that an African American is getting an advantage in landing a good job or a spot in a good college because of an injustice that they themselves never committed, when they're told that their fears about crime in urban neighborhoods are somehow prejudiced, resentment builds over time.

Like the anger within the black community, these resentments aren't always expressed in polite company. But they have helped shape the political landscape for at least a generation. Anger over welfare and affirmative action helped forge the Reagan Coalition. Politicians routinely exploited fears of crime for their own electoral ends. Talk-show hosts and conservative commentators built entire careers unmasking bogus claims of racism while dismissing legitimate discussions of racial injustice and inequality as mere political correctness or reverse racism.

Just as black anger often proved counterproductive, so have these white resentments distracted attention from the real culprits of the middle-class squeeze—a corporate culture rife with inside dealing, questionable accounting practices, and short-term greed; a Washington dominated by lobbyists and special interests; economic policies that favor the few over the many. And yet, to wish away the resentments of white Americans, to label them as misguided or even racist, without recognizing they are grounded in legitimate concerns— this, too, widens the racial divide, and blocks the path to understanding.

This is where we are right now. It's a racial stalemate we've been stuck in for years. Contrary to the claims of some of my critics, black and white, I have never been so naive as to believe that we can get beyond our racial divisions in a single election cycle, or with a single candidacy—particularly a candidacy as imperfect as my own.

But I have asserted a firm conviction—a conviction rooted in my faith in God and my faith in the American people—that working together we can move beyond some of our old racial wounds, and that in fact we have no choice if we are to continue on the path of a more perfect union.

For the African-American community, that path means embracing the burdens of our past without becoming victims of our past. It means continuing to insist on a full measure of justice in every aspect of American life. But it also means binding our particular grievances—for better health care, and better schools, and better jobs—to the larger aspirations of all Americans—the white woman struggling to break the glass ceiling, the white man who has been laid off, the immigrant trying to feed his family. And it means taking full responsibility for our own lives—by demanding more from our fathers, and spending more time with our children, and reading to them, and teaching them that while they may face challenges and discrimination in their own lives, they must never succumb to despair or cynicism; they must always believe that they can write their own destiny.

Ironically, this quintessentially American—and yes, conservative—notion of self-help found frequent expression in Reverend Wright's sermons. But what my former pastor too often failed to understand is that embarking on a program of self-help also requires a belief that society can change.

The profound mistake of Reverend Wright's sermons is not that he spoke about racism in our society. It's that he spoke as if our society was static; as if no progress has been made; as if this country—a country that has made it possible for one of his own members to run for the highest office in the land and build a coalition of white and black, Latino and Asian, rich and poor, young and old—is still irrevocably bound to a tragic past. But what we know—what we have seen—is that America can change. That is the true genius of this nation. What we have already achieved gives us hope—the audacity to hope—for what we can and must achieve tomorrow.

In the white community, the path to a more perfect union means acknowledging that what ails the African-American community does not just exist in the minds of black people; that the legacy of discrimination and current incidents of discrimination—while less overt than in the past—are real and must be addressed. Not just with words, but with deeds—by investing in our schools and our communities; by enforcing our civil rights laws and ensuring fairness in our criminal justice system; by providing this generation with ladders of opportunity that were unavailable for previous generations. It requires all Americans to realize that your dreams do not have to come at the expense of my dreams; that investing in the health, welfare, and education of black and brown and white children will ultimately help all of America prosper.

In the end, then, what is called for is nothing more, and nothing less, than what all the world's great religions demand—that we do unto others as we would have them do unto us. Let us be our brother's keeper, Scripture tells us. Let us be our sister's keeper. Let us find that common stake we all have in one another, and let our politics reflect that spirit as well.

For we have a choice in this country. We can accept a politics that breeds division, and conflict, and cynicism. We can tackle race only as spectacle, as we did in the OJ trial—or in the wake of tragedy, as we did in the aftermath of Katrina—or as fodder for the nightly news. We can play Reverend Wright's sermons on every channel, every day, and talk about them from now until the election, and make the only question in this campaign whether or not the American people think that I somehow believe or sympathize with his most offensive words. We can pounce on some gaffe by a Hillary supporter as evidence that she's playing the race card, or we can speculate on whether white men will all flock to John McCain in the general election regardless of his policies.

We can do that.

But if we do, I can tell you that in the next election, we'll be talking about some other distraction. And then another one. And then another one. And nothing will change.

That is one option. Or, at this moment, in this election, we can come together and say, "Not this time." This time we want to talk about the crumbling schools that are stealing the future of black children and white children and Asian children and Hispanic children and Native American children. This time we want to reject the cynicism that tells us that these kids can't learn; that those kids who don't look like us are somebody else's problem. The children of America are not those kids, they are our kids, and we will not let them fall behind in a twenty-first-century economy. Not this time.

This time we want to talk about how the lines in the emergency room are filled with whites and blacks and Hispanics who do not have health care, who don't have the power on their own to overcome the special interests in Washington, but who can take them on if we do it together.

This time we want to talk about the shuttered mills that once provided a decent life for men and women of every race, and the homes for sale that once belonged to Americans from every religion, every region, every walk of life. This time we want to talk about the fact that the real problem is not that someone who doesn't look like you might take your job; it's that the corporation you work for will ship it overseas for nothing more than a profit.

This time we want to talk about the men and women of every color and creed who serve together, and fight together, and bleed together under the same proud flag. We want to talk about how to bring them home from a war that never should've been authorized and never should've been waged, and we want to talk about how we'll show our patriotism by caring for them, and their families, and giving them the benefits they have earned.

I would not be running for President if I didn't believe with all my heart that this is what the vast majority of Americans want for this country. This union may never be perfect, but generation after generation has shown that it can always be perfected. And today, whenever I find myself feeling doubtful or cynical about this possibility, what gives me the most hope is the next generation—the young people whose attitudes and beliefs and openness to change have already made history in this election.

There is one story in particular that I'd like to leave you with today—a story I told when I had the great honor of speaking on Dr. King's birthday at his home church, Ebenezer Baptist, in Atlanta.

There is a young, twenty-three-year-old white woman named Ashley Baia who organized for our campaign in Florence, South Carolina. She had been working to organize a mostly African-American community since the beginning of this campaign, and one day she was at a round-table discussion where everyone went around telling their stories and why they were there.

And Ashley said that when she was nine years old, her mother got cancer. And because she had to miss days of work, she was let go and lost her health care. They had to file for bankruptcy, and that's when Ashley decided that she had to do something to help her mom.

She knew that food was one of their most expensive costs, and so Ashley convinced her mother that what she really liked and really wanted to eat more than anything else was mustard and relish sandwiches. Because that was the cheapest way to eat.

She did this for a year until her mom got better, and she told everyone at the round table that the reason she joined our campaign was so that she could help the millions of other children in the country who want and need to help their parents, too.

Now Ashley might have made a different choice. Perhaps somebody told her along the way that the source of her mother's problems were blacks who were on welfare and too lazy to work, or Hispanics who were coming into the country illegally. But she didn't. She sought out allies in her fight against injustice.

Anyway, Ashley finishes her story and then goes around the room and asks everyone else why they're supporting the campaign. They all have different stories and reasons. Many bring up a specific issue. And finally they come to this elderly black man who's been sitting there quietly the entire time. And Ashley asks him why he's there. And he does not bring up a specific issue. He does not say health care or the economy. He does not say education or the war. He does not say that he was there because of Barack Obama. He simply says to everyone in the room, "I am here because of Ashley."

"I am here because of Ashley." By itself, that single moment of recognition between that young white girl and that old black man is not enough. It is not enough to give health care to the sick, or jobs to the jobless, or education to our children.

But it is where we start. It is where our union grows stronger. And as so many generations have come to realize over the course of the two hundred and twenty-one years since a band of patriots signed that document in Philadelphia, that is where the perfection begins.

FATHER'S DAY 2008

June 15, 2008 | Apostolic Church of God | Chicago, Illinois

GOOD MORNING. It's good to be home on this Father's Day with my girls, and it's an honor to spend some time with all of you today in the house of our Lord.

At the end of the Sermon on the Mount, Jesus closes by saying, "Whoever hears these words of mine, and does them, shall be likened to a wise man who built his house upon a rock: and the rain descended, and the floods came, and the winds blew, and beat upon that house, and it fell not, for it was founded upon a rock." [Matthew 7:24–25]

Here at Apostolic, you are blessed to worship in a house that has been founded on the rock of Jesus Christ, our Lord and Savior. But it is also built on another rock, another foundation—and that rock is Bishop Arthur Brazier. In forty-eight years, he has built this congregation from just a few hundred to more than twenty thousand strong—a congregation that, because of his leadership, has braved the fierce winds and heavy rains of violence and poverty; joblessness and hopelessness. Because of his work and his ministry, there are more graduates and fewer gang members in the neighborhoods surrounding this church. There are more homes and fewer homeless. There is more community and less chaos because Bishop Brazier continued the march for justice that he began by Dr. King's side all those years ago. He is the reason this house has stood tall for half a century. And on this Father's Day, it must make him proud to know that the man now charged with keeping its foundation strong is his son and your new pastor, Reverend Byron Brazier.

Of all the rocks upon which we build our lives, we are reminded today that family is the most important. And we are called to recognize and honor how critical every father is to that foundation. They are teachers and coaches. They are mentors and role models. They are examples of success and the men who constantly push us toward it.

But if we are honest with ourselves, we'll admit that what too many fathers also are is missing—missing from too many lives and too many homes. They have abandoned their responsibilities, acting like boys instead of men. And the foundations of our families are weaker because of it.

You and I know how true this is in the African-American community. We know that more than half of all black children live in single-parent households, a number that has doubled—doubled—since we were children. We know the statistics—that children who grow up without a father are five times more likely to live in poverty and commit crime; nine times more likely to drop out of schools; and twenty times more likely to end up in prison. They are more likely to have behavioral problems, or run away from home, or become teenage parents themselves. And the foundations of our community are weaker because of it.

How many times in the last year has this city lost a child at the hands of another child? How many times have our hearts stopped in the middle of the night with the sound of a gunshot or a siren? How many teenagers have we seen hanging around on street corners when they should be sitting in a classroom? How many are sitting in prison when they should be working, or at least looking for a job? How many in this generation are we willing to lose to poverty or violence or addiction? How many?

Yes, we need more cops on the street. Yes, we need fewer guns in the hands of people who shouldn't have them. Yes, we need more money for our schools, and more outstanding teachers in the classroom, and more after-school programs for our children. Yes, we need more jobs and more job training and more opportunity in our communities.

But we also need families to raise our children. We need fathers to realize that responsibility does not end at conception. We need them to realize that what makes you a man is not the ability to have a child—it's the courage to raise one.

We need to help all the mothers out there who are raising these kids by themselves; the mothers who drop them off at school, go to work, pick them up in the afternoon, work another shift, get dinner, make lunches, pay the bills, fix the house, and all the other things it takes both parents to do. So many of these women are doing a heroic job, but they need support. They need another parent. Their children need another parent. That's what keeps their foundation strong. It's what keeps the foundation of our country strong.

I know what it means to have an absent father, although my circumstances weren't as tough as they are for many young people today. Even though my father left us when I was two years old, and I only knew him from the letters he wrote and the stories that my family told, I was luckier than most. I grew up in Hawaii, and had two wonderful grandparents from Kansas who poured everything they had into helping my mother raise my sister and me—who worked with her to teach us about love and respect and the obligations we have to one another. I screwed up more often than I should've, but I got plenty of second chances. And even though we didn't have a lot of money, scholarships gave me the opportunity to go to some of the best schools in the country. A lot of kids don't get these chances today. There is no margin for error in their lives. So my own story is different in that way.

Still, I know the toll that being a single parent took on my mother—how she struggled at times to pay the bills; to give us the things that other kids had; to play all the roles that both parents are supposed to play. And I know the toll it took on me. So I resolved many years ago that it was my obligation to break the cycle—that if I could be anything in life, I would be a good father to my girls; that if I could give them anything, I would give them that rock—that foundation— on which to build their lives. And that would be the greatest gift I could offer.

I say this knowing that I have been an imperfect father— knowing that I have made mistakes and will continue to make more; wishing that I could be home for my girls and my wife more than I am right now. I say this knowing all of these things because even as we are imperfect, even as we face difficult circumstances, there are still certain lessons we must strive to live and learn as fathers—whether we are black or white; rich or poor; from the South Side or the wealthiest suburb.

The first is setting an example of excellence for our children—because if we want to set high expectations for them, we've got to set high expectations for ourselves. It's great if you have a job; it's even better if you have a college degree. It's a wonderful thing if you are married and living in a home with your children, but don't just sit in the house and watch *SportsCenter* all weekend long. That's why so many children are growing up in front of the television. As fathers and parents, we've got to spend more time with them, and help them with their homework, and replace the video game or the remote control with a book once in a while. That's how we build that foundation.

We know that education is everything to our children's future. We know that they will no longer just compete for good jobs with children from Indiana, but children from India and China and all over the world. We know the work and the studying and the level of education that requires.

You know, sometimes I'll go to an eighth-grade graduation and there's all that pomp and circumstance and gowns and flowers. And I think to myself, It's just eighth grade. To really compete, they need to graduate high school, and then they need to graduate college, and they probably need a graduate degree, too. An eighth-grade education doesn't cut it today. Let's give them a handshake and tell them to get their butts back in the library!

It's up to us—as fathers and parents—to instill this ethic of excellence in our children. It's up to us to say to our daughters, don't ever let images on TV tell you what you are worth, because I expect you to dream without limit and reach for those goals. It's up to us to tell our sons, those songs on the radio may glorify violence, but in my house we give glory to achievement, self-respect, and hard work. It's up to us to set these high expectations. And that means meeting those expectations ourselves. That means setting examples of excellence in our own lives.

The second thing we need to do as fathers is pass along the value of empathy to our children. Not sympathy, but empathy—the ability to stand in somebody else's shoes; to look at the world through their eyes. Sometimes it's so easy to get caught up in "us," that we forget about our obligations to one another. There's a culture in our society that says remembering these obligations is somehow soft—that we can't show weakness, and so therefore we can't show kindness.

But our young boys and girls see that. They see when you are ignoring or mistreating your wife. They see when you are inconsiderate at home; or when you are distant; or when you are thinking only of yourself. And so it's no surprise when we see that behavior in our schools or on our streets. That's why we pass on the values of empathy and kindness to our children by living them. We need to show our kids that you're not strong by putting other people down—you're strong by lifting them up. That's our responsibility as fathers.

And by the way—it's a responsibility that also extends to Washington. Because if fathers are doing their part; if they're taking their responsibilities seriously to be there for their children, and set high expectations for them, and instill in them a sense of excellence and empathy, then our government should meet them halfway.

We should be making it easier for fathers who make responsible choices and harder for those who avoid them. We should get rid of the financial penalties we impose on married couples right now and start making sure that every dime of child support goes directly to helping children instead of some bureaucrat. We should reward fathers who pay that child support with job training and job opportunities and a larger Earned Income Tax Credit that can help them pay the bills. We should expand programs where registered nurses visit expectant and new mothers and help them learn how to care for themselves before the baby is born and what to do after—programs that have helped increase father involvement, women's employment, and children's readiness for school. We should help these new families care for their children by expanding maternity and paternity leave, and we should guarantee every worker more paid sick leave so they can stay home to take care of their child without losing their income.

We should take all of these steps to build a strong foundation for our children. But we should also know that even if we do; even if we meet our obligations as fathers and parents; even if Washington does its part, too, we will still face difficult challenges in our lives. There will still be days of struggle and heartache. The rains will still come and the winds will still blow.

And that is why the final lesson we must learn as fathers

is also the greatest gift we can pass on to our children—and that is the gift of hope.

I'm not talking about an idle hope that's little more than blind optimism or willful ignorance of the problems we face. I'm talking about hope as that spirit inside us that insists, despite all evidence to the contrary, that something better is waiting for us if we're willing to work for it and fight for it. If we are willing to believe.

I was answering questions at a town hall meeting in Wisconsin the other day and a young man raised his hand, and I figured he'd ask about college tuition or energy or maybe the war in Iraq. But instead he looked at me very seriously and he asked, "What does life mean to you?"

Now, I have to admit that I wasn't quite prepared for that one. I think I stammered for a little bit, but then I stopped and gave it some thought, and I said this:

When I was a young man, I thought life was all about me—how do I make my way in the world, and how do I become successful and how do I get the things that I want.

But now, my life revolves around my two little girls. And what I think about is what kind of world I'm leaving them. Are they living in a country where there's a huge gap between a few who are wealthy and a whole bunch of people who are struggling every day? Are they living in a country that is still divided by race? A country where, because they're girls, they don't have as much opportunity as boys do? Are they living in a country where we are hated around the world because we don't cooperate effectively with other nations? Are they living in a world that is in grave danger because of what we've done to its climate?

And what I've realized is that life doesn't count for much unless you're willing to do your small part to leave our children—all of our children—a better world. Even if it's difficult. Even if the work seems great. Even if we don't get very far in our lifetime.

That is our ultimate responsibility as fathers and parents. We try. We hope. We do what we can to build our house upon the sturdiest rock. And when the winds come, and the rains fall, and they beat upon that house, we keep faith that our Father will be there to guide us, and watch over us, and protect us, and lead His children through the darkest of storms into the light of a better day. That is my prayer for all of us on this Father's Day, and that is my hope for this country in the years ahead. May God bless you and your children. Thank you.

RENEWING AMERICAN
COMPETITIVENESS

June 16, 2008 | *Flint, Michigan*

IT'S GREAT to be at Kettering—a university that is teaching the next generation of leaders and training workers to have the skills they need to advance their own careers and communities.

For months, the state of our economy has dominated the headlines—and the news hasn't been good. The subprime lending debacle has sent the housing market into a tailspin and caused a broader contraction in the credit markets. Over 360,000 jobs have been lost this year, with the unemployment rate registering the biggest one-month jump since February 1986. Incomes have failed to keep pace with the rising costs of health insurance and college, and record oil and food prices have left families struggling just to keep up.

Of course, grim economic news is nothing new to Flint. Manufacturing jobs have been leaving here for decades now. The jobs that have replaced them pay less and offer fewer, if any, benefits. Hardworking Americans who could once count on a single paycheck to support their families have not only lost jobs, but their health care and their pensions as well. Worst of all, many have lost confidence in that fundamental American promise that our children will have a better life than we do.

So these are challenging times. That's why I spent last week talking about immediate steps we need to take to provide working Americans with relief. A broad-based, middle-class tax cut, to help offset the rising cost of gas and food. A foreclosure prevention fund, to help stabilize the housing market. A health care plan that lowers costs and gives those without health insurance the same kind of coverage members of Congress have. A commitment to retirement security that stabilizes Social Security and provides workers a means to increase savings. And a plan to crack down on unfair and sometimes deceptive lending in the credit card and housing markets, to help families climb out of crippling debt and stay out of debt in the first place.

These steps are all paid for and designed to restore balance and fairness to the American economy after years of Bush Administration policies that tilted the playing field in favor of the wealthy and the well-connected. But the truth is, none of these short-term steps alone will ensure America's future. Yes, we have to make sure that the economic pie is sliced more fairly, but we also have to make sure that the economic pie is growing. Yes, we need to provide immediate help to families who are struggling in places like Flint, but we also need a serious plan to create new jobs and industry.

We can't simply return to the strategies of the past. For we are living through an age of fundamental economic transformation. Technology has changed the way we live

and the way the world does business. The collapse of the Soviet Union and the advance of capitalism have vanquished
old challenges to America's global leadership, but new challenges have emerged, from China and India, Eastern Europe
and Brazil. Jobs and industries can move to any country with
an Internet connection and willing workers. Michigan's children will grow up facing competition not just from California or South Carolina, but also from Beijing and Bangalore.

A few years ago, I saw a picture of this new reality during
a visit to Google's headquarters in California. Toward the
end of my tour, I was brought into a room where a three-
dimensional image of the earth rotated on a large flat-panel
monitor. Across this image, there were countless lights in
different colors. A young engineer explained that the lights
represented all of the Internet searches taking place across
the world, and each color represented a different language.
The image was mesmerizing—a picture of a world where old
boundaries are disappearing; a world where communication,
connection, and competition can come from anywhere.

There are some who believe that we must try to turn
back the clock on this new world; that the only chance to
maintain our living standards is to build a fortress around
America; to stop trading with other countries, shut down
immigration, and rely on old industries. I disagree. Not only
is it impossible to turn back the tide of globalization, but
efforts to do so can make us worse off.

Rather than fear the future, we must embrace it. I have
no doubt that America can compete—and succeed—in the
twenty-first century. And I know as well that, more than
anything else, success will depend not on our government,

but on the dynamism, determination, and innovation of the American people. Here in Flint, it was the private sector that helped turn lumber into the wagons that sent this country west; that built the tanks that faced down Fascism; and that turned out the automobiles that were the cornerstone of America's manufacturing boom.

But at critical moments of transition like this one, success has also depended on national leadership that moved the country forward with confidence and a common purpose. That's what our Founding Fathers did after winning independence, when they tied together the economies of the thirteen states and created the American market. That's what Lincoln did in the midst of the Civil War, when he pushed for a transcontinental railroad, incorporated our National Academy of Sciences, passed the Homestead Act, and created our system of land grant colleges. That's what FDR did in confronting capitalism's gravest crisis, when he forged the social safety net, built the Hoover Dam, created the Tennessee Valley Authority, and invested in an Arsenal of Democracy. And that's what Kennedy did in the dark days of the Cold War, when he called us to a new frontier, created the Apollo program, and put us on a pathway to the moon.

This was leadership that had the strength to turn moments of adversity into opportunity, the wisdom to see a little further down the road, and the courage to challenge conventional thinking and worn ideas so that we could reinvent our economy to seize the future. That's not the kind of leadership that we have seen out of Washington recently. But that's the kind of leadership I intend to provide as President of the United States.

These past eight years will be remembered for misguided policies, missed opportunities, and a rigid and ideological adherence to discredited ideas. Almost a decade into this century, we still have no real strategy to compete in a global economy. Just think of what we could have done. We could have made a real commitment to a world-class education for our kids, but instead we passed No Child Left Behind, a law that—however well intended—left the money behind and alienated teachers and principals instead of inspiring them. We could have done something to end our addiction to oil, but instead we continued down a path that funds both sides of the war on terror, endangers our planet, and has left Americans struggling with $4-a-gallon gasoline. We could have invested in innovation and rebuilt our crumbling roads and bridges, but instead we've spent hundreds of billions of dollars fighting a war in Iraq that should've never been authorized and never been waged.

Worse yet, the price tag for these failures is being passed to our children. The Clinton Administration left behind a surplus, but this Administration squandered it. We face budget deficits in the hundreds of billions and are nearly $10 trillion in debt. We've borrowed billions from countries like China to finance needless tax cuts for the wealthiest Americans and an unnecessary war, and yet Senator McCain is explicitly running to continue and expand these policies, without a realistic plan to pay for it.

The pundits talk about two debates—one on national security and one on the economy—but they miss the point. We didn't win the Cold War just because of the strength of our military. We also prevailed because of the vigor of our economy and the endurance of our ideals. In this century, we won't be secure if we bankroll terrorists and dictators through our dependence on oil. We won't be safe if we can't count on our infrastructure. We won't extend the promise of American greatness unless we invest in our young people and ask them to invest in America.

So there is a clear choice in this election. Instead of reaching for new horizons, George Bush has put us in a hole, and John McCain's policies will keep us there. I want to take us in a new and better direction. I reject the belief that we should either shrink from the challenge of globalization, or fall back on the same tired and failed approaches of the last eight years. It's time for new policies that create the jobs and opportunities of the future—a competitiveness agenda built upon education and energy, innovation and infrastructure, fair trade and reform.

This agenda starts with education. Whether you're conservative or liberal, Republican or Democrat, practically every economist agrees that in this digital age, a highly educated and skilled workforce will be the key not only to individual opportunity, but to the overall success of our economy as well. We cannot be satisfied until every child in America— and I mean every child—has the same chances for a good education that we want for our own children.

And yet, despite this consensus, we continually fail to deliver. A few years ago, I visited a high school outside Chicago. The number one concern I heard from those students was that the school district couldn't afford to keep teachers for a full day, so school let out at one-thirty every afternoon. That cut out critical classes like science and labs. Imagine that—these kids wanted more school. They knew they were being shortchanged. Unfortunately, stories like this can be found across America. Only 20 percent of students are prepared to take college classes in English, math, and science. We have one of the highest dropout rates of any industrialized nation, and barely one-tenth of our low-income students will graduate from college. That will cripple their ability to keep pace in this global economy and compromise our ability to compete as a nation.

Senator McCain doesn't talk about education much. But I don't accept the status quo. It is morally unacceptable and economically untenable. It's time to make a historic commitment to education—a real commitment that will require new resources and new reforms.

We can start by investing $10 billion to guarantee access to quality, affordable, early childhood education for every child in America. Every dollar that we spend on these programs puts our children on a path to success, while saving us as much as $10 in reduced health care costs, crime, and welfare later on.

We can fix the failures of No Child Left Behind, while focusing on accountability. That means providing the funding that was promised. More importantly, it means reaching high standards, but not by relying on a single, high-stakes standardized test that distorts how teachers teach. Instead, we need to work with governors, educators, and especially teachers to develop better assessment tools that effectively measure student achievement and encourage the kinds of research, scientific investigation, and problem solving that our children will need to compete.

And we need to recruit an army of new teachers. I'll make this pledge as President—if you commit your life to teaching, America will pay for your college education. We'll recruit teachers in math and science, and deploy them to understaffed school districts in our inner cities and rural America. We'll expand mentoring programs that pair experienced teachers with new recruits. And when our teachers succeed, I won't just talk about how great they are—I'll reward their greatness with better pay and more support.

But research shows that resources alone won't create the schools that we need to help our children succeed. We also need to encourage innovation—by adopting curricula and the school calendar to the needs of the twenty-first century; by updating the schools of education that produce most of our teachers; by welcoming charter schools within the public schools system; and streamlining the certification process for engineers or businesspeople who want to shift careers and teach.

We must also challenge the system that prevents us from promoting and rewarding excellence in teaching. We cannot ask our teachers to perform the impossible—to teach poorly prepared children with inadequate resources—and then punish them when children perform poorly on a standardized test. But if we give teachers the resources they need; if we pay them more and give them time for professional development; if they are given ownership over the design of better assessment tools and a creative curricula; if we shape reforms with teachers rather than imposing changes on teachers, then it is fair to expect better results. Where there are teachers who are still struggling and underperforming, we should provide them with individual help and support. And if they're still underperforming after that, we should find a quick and fair way to put another teacher in that classroom. Our children deserve no less.

Finally, our commitment cannot end with a high-school degree. The chance to get a college education must not be a privilege of the few—it should be a birthright of every single American. Senator McCain is campaigning on a plan to give more tax breaks to corporations. I want to give tax breaks to young people, in the form of an annual $4,000 tax credit that will cover two-thirds of the tuition at an average public college and make community college completely free. In return, I will ask students to serve, whether it's by teaching, joining the Peace Corps, or working in your community. And for those who serve in our military, we'll cover all of your tuition with an even more generous twenty-first-century GI Bill. The idea is simple—America invests in you, and you invest in America. That's how we're going to ensure that America succeeds in this century.

Reforming our education system will require sustained effort from all of us—parents and teachers; federal, state, and local governments. The same is true for the second leg of our competitiveness agenda—a bold and sustainable energy policy.

In the past, America has been stirred to action when a new challenge threatened our national security. That was true when German and Japanese armies advanced across Europe and Asia, or when the Soviets launched *Sputnik*. The energy threat we face today may be less direct, but it is real. Our dependence on foreign oil strains family budgets and saps our economy. Oil money pays for the bombs going off from Baghdad to Beirut, and the bombast of dictators from Caracas to Tehran. Our nation will not be secure unless we take that leverage away, and our planet will not be safe unless we move decisively toward a clean-energy future.

The dangers are eclipsed only by the opportunities that would come with change. We know the jobs of the twenty-first century will be created in developing alternative energy. The question is whether these jobs will be created in America or abroad. Already, we've seen countries like Germany, Spain, and Brazil reap the benefits of economic growth from clean energy. But we are decades behind in confronting this challenge. George Bush has spent most of his Administration denying that we have a problem and making deals with Big Oil behind closed doors. And while John McCain deserves credit for speaking out against the threat of climate change, his rhetoric is undercut by a record of voting time and again against important investments in renewable energy.

It's time to make energy security a leading priority. My energy plan will invest $150 billion over the next ten years to establish a green energy sector that will create up to five million jobs over the next two decades. Good jobs, like the ones I saw in Pennsylvania where workers make wind turbines, or the jobs that will be created when plug-in hybrids or electric cars start rolling off the assembly line here in Michigan. We'll help manufacturers—particularly in the auto industry—convert to green technology and help workers learn the skills they need. And unlike George Bush, I won't wait until the sixth year of my presidency to sit down with the automakers. I'll meet with them during my campaign, and I'll meet with them as President to talk about how we're going to build the cars of the future right here in Michigan.

And when I'm President, we will invest in research and development of every form of alternative energy—solar, wind, and biofuels, as well as technologies that can make coal clean and nuclear power safe. We will provide incentives to businesses and consumers to save energy and make buildings more efficient. That's how we're going to create jobs that pay well and can't be outsourced. That's how we're going to win back control of our own destiny from oil-rich dictators. And that's how we'll solve the problem of $4-a-gallon gas—not with another Washington gimmick like John McCain's gas-tax holiday that would pad oil company profits while draining the highway fund that Michigan depends on.

Moreover, our commitment to manufacturing cannot end with green jobs. That's why I'll end tax breaks that ship jobs overseas, and invest in American jobs. Senator McCain has a different view. He's voted to keep tax incentives that encourage companies to move abroad. He should listen to leaders in Michigan like Carl Levin, who have put forward serious proposals to address the crisis in manufacturing. We need to support programs like Michigan's 21st Century Jobs Fund and build on best practices across the country. That's why I'll create an Advanced Manufacturing Fund to invest in places hit hard by job loss. I'll partner with community colleges, so that we're training workers to meet the demands of local industry.

And we can't just focus on preserving existing industries. We have to be in the business of encouraging new ones—and that means science, research, and technology. For two centuries, America led the world in innovation. But this Administration's hostility to science has taken a toll. At a time when technology is shaping our future, we devote a smaller and smaller share of our national resources to research and development. It's time for America to lead. I'll double federal funding for basic research, and make the R&D tax credit permanent. We can ensure that the discoveries of the twenty-first century happen in America—in our labs and universities; at places like Kettering and the University of Michigan; Wayne State and Michigan State.

Encouraging new industry also means giving more support to American entrepreneurs. The other day, Senator McCain gave a speech to the Small Business Summit, where he attacked my plan to provide tax relief for the middle class. What he didn't say is that I've also proposed exempting all start-up companies from capital gains taxes. In other words, John McCain would tax them. I won't. We'll work, at every juncture, to remove bureaucratic barriers for small and start-up businesses—for example, by making the patent process more efficient and reliable. And we'll help with technical support to do everything we can to make sure the next Google or Microsoft is started here in America.

And we know that America won't be able to compete if skyrocketing costs cause companies like the Big Three to spend $1,500 on health care for every car, and condemn millions of Americans to the risk of no coverage. That's why we need to commit ourselves to electronic medical records that enhance care while lowering costs. We need to invest in biomedical research and stem cell research, so that we're at the leading edge of prevention and treatment. And we need to finally pass universal health care so that every American has access to health insurance that they can afford, and are getting the preventive services that are the key to cutting health care costs. That's what I pledge to do in my first term as President.

A third part of our agenda must be a commitment to twenty-first-century infrastructure. If we want to keep up with China or Europe, we can't settle for crumbling roads and bridges, aging water and sewer pipes, and faltering electrical grids that cost us billions in blackouts, repairs, and travel delays. It's gotten so bad that the American Society of Civil Engineers gave our national infrastructure a "D." A century ago, Teddy Roosevelt called together leaders from business and government to develop a plan for twentieth-century infrastructure. It falls to us to do the same.

As President, I will launch a National Infrastructure Reinvestment Bank that will invest $60 billion over ten years—a bank that can leverage private investment in infrastructure improvements and create nearly two million new jobs. The work will be determined by what will maximize our safety and security and ability to compete. We will fund this bank as we bring the war in Iraq to a responsible close. It's time to stop spending billions of dollars a week on a blank check for an Iraqi government that won't spend its own oil revenues. It's time to strengthen transportation and to protect vulnerable targets from terrorism at home. We can modernize our power grid, which will help conservation and spur on the development and distribution of clean energy. We can invest in rail, so that cities like Detroit, Chicago, Milwaukee, and St. Louis are connected by high-speed trains, and folks have alternatives to air travel. That's what we can do if we commit to rebuild a stronger America.

As part of this commitment to infrastructure, we need to upgrade our digital superhighway as well. When I looked at that map of the world mounted on the screen at Google, I was struck at first by the light generated by Internet searches coming from every corner of the earth. But then I was struck by the darkness. Huge chunks of Africa and parts of Asia where the light of the information revolution has yet to shine. And then I noticed portions of the United States where the thick cords of light dissolved into a few discrete strands.

It is unacceptable that here, in the country that invented the Internet, we fell to fifteenth in the world in broadband deployment. When kids in downtown Flint or rural Iowa can't afford or access high-speed Internet, that sets back America's ability to compete. As President, I will set a simple goal: every American should have the highest speed broadband access—no matter where you live or how much money you have. We'll connect schools, libraries, and hospitals. And we'll take on special interests to unleash the power of wireless spectrum for our safety and connectivity.

A revamped education system. A bold new energy strategy. A more efficient health care system. Renewed investment in basic research and our infrastructure. These are the pillars of a more competitive economy that will take advantage of the global marketplace's opportunities.

But even as we welcome competition, we need to remember that our economic policies must be supported by strong and smart trade policies. I have said before, and will say again—I believe in free trade. It can save money for our consumers, generate business for U.S. exporters, and expand global wealth. But unlike George Bush and John McCain, I do not think that any trade agreement is a good trade agreement. I don't think an agreement that allows South Korea to export hundreds of thousands of cars into the United States, but continues to restrict U.S. car exports into South Korea to a few thousand, is a smart deal. I don't think that trade agreements without labor or environmental agreements are in our long-term interests.

If we continue to let our trade policy be dictated by special interests, then American workers will continue to be undermined, and public support for robust trade will continue to erode. That might make sense to the Washington lobbyists who run Senator McCain's campaign, but it won't help our nation compete. Allowing subsidized and unfairly traded products to flood our markets is not free trade and it's not fair to the people of Michigan. We cannot stand by while countries manipulate currencies to promote exports, creating huge imbalances in the global economy. We cannot let foreign regulatory policies exclude American products. We cannot let enforcement of existing trade agreements take a backseat to the negotiation of new ones. Put simply, we need tougher negotiators on our side of the table—to strike bargains that are good not just for Wall Street, but also for Main Street. And when I am President, that's what we will do.

Finally, let me say a word about fiscal responsibility. I recognize that my agenda is ambitious—particularly in light of Bush Administration fiscal policies that have run up the national debt by over $4 trillion. Entitlement spending is bound to increase as the baby boom generation retires.

But the answer to our fiscal problems is not to continue to shortchange investments in education, energy, innovation, and infrastructure—investments that are vital to long-term growth. Instead, we need to end the Iraq War, eliminate waste in existing government programs, generate revenue by charging polluters for the greenhouse gases they are sending into our atmosphere—and put an end to the reckless, special-interest-driven corporate loopholes and tax cuts for the wealthy that have been the centerpiece of the Bush Administration's economic policy.

John McCain wants to double down on George Bush's disastrous policies—not only by making permanent the Bush tax cuts for the wealthy, but by $300 billion in new tax cuts that give a quarter of their revenue to households making over $2.8 million. Worse yet, he hasn't detailed how he would pay for this new giveaway. There is nothing fiscally conservative about this approach. It will continue to drive up deficits, force us to borrow massively from foreign countries, and shift the burden onto working people today and our children tomorrow. Meanwhile, John McCain will shortchange investments in education, energy, and innovation, making the next generation of Americans less able to compete. That's unacceptable. It's time to make tough choices so that we have a smarter government that pays its way and makes the right investments for America's future.

It falls to us to shape a new century. Every aspect of our government should be under review. We can ill afford needless layers of bureaucracy and outmoded programs. My Administration will open up the doors of democracy. We'll put government data online and use technology to shine a light on spending. We'll invite the service and participation of American citizens and cut through the red tape to make sure that every agency is meeting cutting-edge standards. We'll make it clear to the special interests that their days of setting the agenda in Washington are over, because the American people are not the problem in this twenty-first century—they are the answer.

We have a choice. We can continue the Bush status quo—as Senator McCain wants to do—and we will become a country in which few reap the benefits of the global economy, while a growing number work harder for less and depend upon an overburdened public sector. An America in which we run up deficits and expose ourselves to the whims of oil-rich dictators while the opportunities for our children and grandchildren shrink. That is one course we could take.

Or, we can rise together. If we choose to change, just imagine what we can do. The great manufacturers of the twentieth century can turn out cars that run on renewable energy in the twenty-first. Biotechnology labs can find new cures; new rail lines and roadways can connect our communities; goods made here in Michigan can be exported around the world. Our children can get a world-class education, and their dreams of tomorrow can eclipse even our greatest hopes of today.

We can choose to rise together. But it won't be easy. Every one of us will have to work at it by studying harder, training more rigorously, working smarter, and thinking anew. We'll have to slough off bad habits, reform our institutions, and reengage the world. We can do that, because this is America—a country that has been defined by a determination to believe in, and work for, things unseen.

Every so often, there are times when America must rise to meet a moment. So it has been for the generations that built the railroads and beat back the Depression; that worked on the first assembly line and that went to the moon. So it must be for us today. This is our moment. This is our time to unite in common purpose, to make this century the next American century. Because when Americans come together, there is no destiny too difficult or too distant for us to reach.

A WORLD THAT
STANDS AS ONE

July 24, 2008 | Berlin, Germany

THANK YOU to the citizens of Berlin and to the people of Germany. Let me thank Chancellor Merkel and Foreign Minister Steinmeier for welcoming me earlier today. Thank you, Mayor Wowereit, the Berlin Senate, the police, and most of all thank you for this welcome.

I come to Berlin as so many of my countrymen have come before. Tonight, I speak to you not as a candidate for President, but as a citizen—a proud citizen of the United States, and a fellow citizen of the world.

I know that I don't look like the Americans who've previously spoken in this great city. The journey that led me here is improbable. My mother was born in the heartland of America, but my father grew up herding goats in Kenya. His father—my grandfather—was a cook, a domestic servant to the British.

At the height of the Cold War, my father decided, like so many others in the forgotten corners of the world, that his yearning—his dream—required the freedom and opportunity promised by the West. And so he wrote letter after letter to universities all across America until somebody, somewhere answered his prayer for a better life.

That is why I'm here. And you are here because you, too, know that yearning. This city, of all cities, knows the dream of freedom. And you know that the only reason we stand here tonight is because men and women from both of our nations came together to work, and struggle, and sacrifice for that better life.

Ours is a partnership that truly began sixty years ago this summer, on the day when the first American plane touched down at Tempelhof.

On that day, much of this continent still lay in ruin. The rubble of this city had yet to be built into a wall. The Soviet shadow had swept across Eastern Europe, while in the West, America, Britain, and France took stock of their losses and pondered how the world might be remade.

This is where the two sides met. And on the twenty-fourth of June, 1948, the communists chose to blockade the western part of the city. They cut off food and supplies to more than two million Germans in an effort to extinguish the last flame of freedom in Berlin.

The size of our forces was no match for the much larger Soviet army. And yet retreat would have allowed Communism to march across Europe. Where the last war had ended, another world war could have easily begun. All that stood in the way was Berlin.

And that's when the airlift began—when the largest and most unlikely rescue in history brought food and hope to the people of this city.

The odds were stacked against success. In the winter, a heavy fog filled the sky above, and many planes were forced to turn back without dropping off the needed supplies. The streets where we stand were filled with hungry families who had no comfort from the cold.

But in the darkest hours, the people of Berlin kept the flame of hope burning. The people of Berlin refused to give up. And on one fall day, hundreds of thousands of Berliners came here, to the Tiergarten, and heard the city's mayor implore the world not to give up on freedom. "There is only one possibility," he said. "For us to stand together united until this battle is won . . . The people of Berlin have spoken. We have done our duty, and we will keep on doing our duty. People of the world: now do your duty . . . People of the world, look at Berlin!"

People of the world—look at Berlin!

Look at Berlin, where Germans and Americans learned to work together and trust each other less than three years after facing each other on the field of battle.

Look at Berlin, where the determination of a people met the generosity of the Marshall Plan and created a German miracle; where a victory over tyranny gave rise to NATO, the greatest alliance ever formed to defend our common security.

Look at Berlin, where the bullet holes in the buildings and the somber stones and pillars near the Brandenburg Gate insist that we never forget our common humanity.

People of the world—look at Berlin, where a wall came down, a continent came together, and history proved that there is no challenge too great for a world that stands as one.

Sixty years after the airlift, we are called upon again. History has led us to a new crossroad, with new promise and new peril. When you, the German people, tore down that wall—a wall that divided East and West; freedom and tyranny; fear and hope—walls came tumbling down around the world. From Kiev to Cape Town, prison camps were closed, and the doors of democracy were opened. Markets opened, too, and the spread of information and technology reduced barriers to opportunity and prosperity. While the twentieth century taught us that we share a common destiny, the twenty-first has revealed a world more intertwined than at any time in human history.

The fall of the Berlin Wall brought new hope. But that very closeness has given rise to new dangers—dangers that cannot be contained within the borders of a country or by the distance of an ocean.

The terrorists of September 11th plotted in Hamburg and trained in Kandahar and Karachi before killing thousands from all over the globe on American soil.

As we speak, cars in Boston and factories in Beijing are melting the ice caps in the Arctic, shrinking coastlines in the Atlantic, and bringing drought to farms from Kansas to Kenya.

Poorly secured nuclear material in the former Soviet Union or secrets from a scientist in Pakistan could help build a bomb that detonates in Paris. The poppies in Afghanistan become the heroin in Berlin. The poverty and violence in Somalia breeds the terror of tomorrow. The genocide in Darfur shames the conscience of us all.

In this new world, such dangerous currents have swept

along faster than our efforts to contain them. That is why we cannot afford to be divided. No one nation, no matter how large or powerful, can defeat such challenges alone. None of us can deny these threats or escape responsibility in meeting them. Yet in the absence of Soviet tanks and a terrible wall, it has become easy to forget this truth. And if we're honest with each other, we know that sometimes, on both sides of the Atlantic, we have drifted apart and forgotten our shared destiny.

In Europe, the view that America is part of what has gone wrong in our world, rather than a force to help make it right, has become all too common. In America, there are voices that deride and deny the importance of Europe's role in our security and our future. Both views miss the truth—that Europeans today are bearing new burdens and taking more responsibility in critical parts of the world; and that just as American bases built in the last century still help to defend the security of this continent, so does our country still sacrifice greatly for freedom around the globe.

Yes, there have been differences between America and Europe. No doubt, there will be differences in the future. But the burdens of global citizenship continue to bind us together. A change of leadership in Washington will not lift this burden. In this new century, Americans and Europeans alike will be required to do more—not less. Partnership and cooperation among nations is not a choice; it is the one way, the only way, to protect our common security and advance our common humanity.

That is why the greatest danger of all is to allow new walls to divide us from one another. The walls between old allies on either side of the Atlantic cannot stand. The walls between the countries with the most and those with the least cannot stand. The walls between races and tribes; natives and immigrants; Christian and Muslim and Jew cannot stand. These now are the walls we must tear down.

We know they have fallen before. After centuries of strife, the people of Europe have formed a union of promise and prosperity. Here, at the base of a column built to mark victory in war, we meet in the center of a Europe at peace. Not only have walls come down in Berlin, but they have come down in Belfast, where Protestant and Catholic found a way to live together; in the Balkans, where our Atlantic alliance ended wars and brought savage war criminals to justice; and in South Africa, where the struggle of a courageous people defeated apartheid.

So history reminds us that walls can be torn down. But the task is never easy. True partnership and true progress requires constant work and sustained sacrifice. They require sharing the burdens of development and diplomacy; of progress and peace. They require allies who will listen to each other, learn from each other, and, most of all, trust each other.

That is why America cannot turn inward. That is why Europe cannot turn inward. America has no better partner than Europe. Now is the time to build new bridges across the globe as strong as the one that bound us across the Atlantic. Now is the time to join together, through constant cooperation, strong institutions, shared sacrifice, and a global commitment to progress, to meet the challenges of the twenty-first century. It was this spirit that led airlift planes to appear in the sky above our heads, and people to assemble where we stand today. And this is the moment when our nations—and all nations—must summon that spirit anew.

This is the moment when we must defeat terror and dry up the well of extremism that supports it. This threat is real and we cannot shrink from our responsibility to combat it. If we could create NATO to face down the Soviet Union, we can join in a new and global partnership to dismantle the networks that have struck in Madrid and Amman; in London and Bali; in Washington and New York. If we could win a battle of ideas against the communists, we can stand with the vast majority of Muslims who reject the extremism that leads to hate instead of hope.

This is the moment when we must renew our resolve to rout the terrorists who threaten our security in Afghanistan, and the traffickers who sell drugs on your streets. No one welcomes war. I recognize the enormous difficulties in Afghanistan. But my country and yours have a stake in seeing that NATO's first mission beyond Europe's borders is a success. For the people of Afghanistan, and for our shared security, the work must be done. America cannot do this alone. The Afghan people need our troops and your troops; our support and your support to defeat the Taliban and Al Qaeda, to develop their economy, and to help them rebuild their nation. We have too much at stake to turn back now.

This is the moment when we must renew the goal of a world without nuclear weapons. The two superpowers that faced each other across the wall of this city came too close too often to destroying all we have built and all that we love. With that wall gone, we need not stand idly by and watch the further spread of the deadly atom. It is time to secure all loose nuclear materials; to stop the spread of nuclear weapons; and to reduce the arsenals from another era. This is the moment to begin the work of seeking the peace of a world without nuclear weapons.

This is the moment when every nation in Europe must have the chance to choose its own tomorrow free from the shadows of yesterday. In this century, we need a strong European Union that deepens the security and prosperity of this continent, while extending a hand abroad. In this century—in this city of all cities—we must reject the Cold War mindset of the past and resolve to work with Russia when we can, to stand up for our values when we must, and to seek a partnership that extends across this entire continent.

This is the moment when we must build on the wealth that open markets have created, and share its benefits more equitably. Trade has been a cornerstone of our growth and global development. But we will not be able to sustain this growth if it favors the few and not the many. Together, we must forge trade that truly rewards the work that creates wealth, with meaningful protections for our people and our planet. This is the moment for trade that is free and fair for all.

This is the moment we must help answer the call for a new dawn in the Middle East. My country must stand with yours and with Europe in sending a direct message to Iran that it must abandon its nuclear ambitions. We must support the Lebanese who have marched and bled for democracy, and the Israelis and Palestinians who seek a secure and lasting peace. And despite past differences, this is the moment when the world should support the millions of Iraqis who seek to rebuild their lives, even as we pass responsibility to the Iraqi government and finally bring this war to a close.

This is the moment when we must come together to save this planet. Let us resolve that we will not leave our children a world where the oceans rise and famine spreads and terrible storms devastate our lands. Let us resolve that all nations— including my own—will act with the same seriousness of purpose as has your nation, and reduce the carbon we send into our atmosphere. This is the moment to give our children back their future. This is the moment to stand as one.

And this is the moment when we must give hope to those left behind in a globalized world. We must remember that the Cold War born in this city was not a battle for land or treasure. Sixty years ago, the planes that flew over Berlin did not drop bombs; instead they delivered food, and coal, and candy to grateful children. And in that show of solidarity, those pilots won more than a military victory. They won hearts and minds; love and loyalty and trust—not just from the people in this city, but from all those who heard the story of what they did here.

Now the world will watch and remember what we do here—what we do with this moment. Will we extend our hand to the people in the forgotten corners of this world who yearn for lives marked by dignity and opportunity; by security and justice? Will we lift the child in Bangladesh from poverty, shelter the refugee in Chad, and banish the scourge of AIDS in our time?

Will we stand for the human rights of the dissident in

Burma, the blogger in Iran, or the voter in Zimbabwe? Will we give meaning to the words "never again" in Darfur?

Will we acknowledge that there is no more powerful example than the one each of our nations projects to the world? Will we reject torture and stand for the rule of law? Will we welcome immigrants from different lands and shun discrimination against those who don't look like us or worship like we do, and keep the promise of equality and opportunity for all of our people?

People of Berlin—people of the world—this is our moment. This is our time.

I know my country has not perfected itself. At times, we've struggled to keep the promise of liberty and equality for all of our people. We've made our share of mistakes, and there are times when our actions around the world have not lived up to our best intentions.

But I also know how much I love America. I know that for more than two centuries, we have strived—at great cost and great sacrifice—to form a more perfect union; to seek, with other nations, a more hopeful world. Our allegiance has never been to any particular tribe or kingdom—indeed, every language is spoken in our country; every culture has left its imprint on ours; every point of view is expressed in our public squares. What has always united us—what has always driven our people, what drew my father to America's shores—is a set of ideals that speak to aspirations shared by all people: that we can live free from fear and free from want; that we can speak our minds and assemble with whomever we choose and worship as we please.

These are the aspirations that joined the fates of all nations in this city. These aspirations are bigger than anything that drives us apart. It is because of these aspirations that the airlift began. It is because of these aspirations that all free people—everywhere—became citizens of Berlin. It is in pursuit of these aspirations that a new generation—our generation—must make our mark on the world.

People of Berlin—and people of the world—the scale of our challenge is great. The road ahead will be long. But I come before you to say that we are heirs to a struggle for freedom. We are a people of improbable hope. With an eye toward the future, with resolve in our hearts, let us remember this history and answer our destiny and remake the world once again.

ELECTION NIGHT

November 4, 2008 | *Chicago, Illinois*

I F THERE is anyone out there who still doubts that America is a place where all things are possible; who still wonders if the dream of our founders is alive in our time; who still questions the power of our democracy, tonight is your answer.

It's the answer told by lines that stretched around schools and churches in numbers this nation has never seen; by people who waited three hours and four hours, many for the first time in their lives, because they believed that this time must be different; that their voices could be that difference.

It's the answer spoken by young and old, rich and poor, Democrat and Republican, black, white, Hispanic, Asian, Native American, gay, straight, disabled and not disabled— Americans who sent a message to the world that we have never been just a collection of individuals or a collection of Red States and Blue States: we are, and always will be, the United States of America.

It's the answer that led those who've been told for so long by so many to be cynical, and fearful, and doubtful about what we can achieve to put their hands on the arc of history and bend it once more toward the hope of a better day.

It's been a long time coming, but tonight, because of what we did on this date, in this election, at this defining moment, change has come to America.

A little bit earlier this evening, I received an extraordinarily gracious call from Senator McCain. Senator McCain fought long and hard in this campaign, and he's fought even longer and harder for the country that he loves. He has endured sacrifices for America that most of us cannot begin to imagine. We are better off for the service rendered by this brave and selfless leader. I congratulate him. I congratulate Governor Palin for all that they've achieved, and I look forward to working with them to renew this nation's promise in the months ahead.

I want to thank my partner in this journey, a man who campaigned from his heart and spoke for the men and women he grew up with on the streets of Scranton and rode with on the train home to Delaware, the Vice President-elect of the United States, Joe Biden.

And I would not be standing here tonight without the unyielding support of my best friend for the last sixteen years, the rock of our family, the love of my life, the nation's next First Lady, Michelle Obama. Sasha and Malia, I love you both more than you can imagine, and you have earned the new puppy that's coming with us to the new White House. And while she's no longer with us, I know my grandmother's watching, along with the family that made me who I am. I miss them tonight. I know that my debt to them is beyond measure.

To my sister Maya, my sister Auma, all my other brothers and sisters, thank you so much for all the support that you've given me. I am grateful to them.

And to my campaign manager, David Plouffe, the unsung hero of this campaign, who built the best—the best political campaign, I think, in the history of the United States of America. To my chief strategist, David Axelrod, who's been a partner with me every step of the way. To the best campaign team ever assembled in the history of politics. You made this happen, and I am forever grateful for what you've sacrificed to get it done.

But above all, I will never forget who this victory truly belongs to—it belongs to you. It belongs to you.

I was never the likeliest candidate for this office. We didn't start with much money or many endorsements. Our campaign was not hatched in the halls of Washington—it began in the backyards of Des Moines and the living rooms of Concord and the front porches of Charleston.

It was built by working men and women who dug into what little savings they had to give five dollars and ten dollars and twenty dollars to the cause. It grew strength from the young people who rejected the myth of their generation's apathy; who left their homes and their families for jobs that offered little pay and less sleep. It drew strength from the not-so-young people who braved the bitter cold and scorching heat to knock on doors of perfect strangers; and from the millions of Americans who volunteered, and organized, and proved that more than two centuries later, a government of the people, by the people, and for the people has not perished from this Earth. This is your victory.

And I know you didn't do this just to win an election, and I know you didn't do it for me. You did it because you understand the enormity of the task that lies ahead. For even as we celebrate tonight, we know the challenges that tomorrow will bring are the greatest of our lifetime—two wars, a planet in peril, the worst financial crisis in a century. Even as we stand here tonight, we know there are brave Americans waking up in the deserts of Iraq and the mountains of Afghanistan to risk their lives for us. There are mothers and fathers who will lie awake after the children fall asleep and wonder how they'll make the mortgage, or pay their doctor's bills, or save enough for their child's college education. There's new energy to harness, new jobs to be created, new schools to build, and threats to meet, alliances to repair.

The road ahead will be long. Our climb will be steep. We may not get there in one year or even in one term, but America—I have never been more hopeful than I am tonight that we will get there. I promise you—we as a people will get there.

There will be setbacks and false starts. There are many who won't agree with every decision or policy I make as President, and we know that government can't solve every problem. But I will always be honest with you about the challenges we face. I will listen to you, especially when we disagree. And above all, I will ask you to join in the work of remaking this nation the only way it's been done in America for 221 years—block by block, brick by brick, calloused hand by calloused hand.

What began twenty-one months ago in the depths of winter cannot end on this autumn night. This victory alone is not the change we seek—it is only the chance for us to make that change. And that cannot happen if we go back to the way things were. It can't happen without you, without a new spirit of service, a new spirit of sacrifice.

So let us summon a new spirit of patriotism, of responsibility, where each of us resolves to pitch in and work harder and look after not only ourselves, but each other. Let us remember that if this financial crisis taught us anything, it's that we cannot have a thriving Wall Street while Main Street suffers—in this country, we rise or fall as one nation; as one people.

Let's resist the temptation to fall back on the same partisanship and pettiness and immaturity that has poisoned our politics for so long. Let's remember that it was a man from this state who first carried the banner of the Republican Party to the White House—a party founded on the values of self-reliance, and individual liberty, and national unity. Those are values that we all share, and while the Democratic Party has won a great victory tonight, we do so with a measure of humility and determination to heal the divides that have held back our progress. As Lincoln said to a nation far more divided than ours, "We are not enemies, but friends . . . though passion may have strained it must not break our bonds of affection." And to those Americans whose support I have yet to earn—I may not have won your vote tonight, but I hear your voices, I need your help, and I will be your President too.

And to all those watching tonight from beyond our shores, from parliaments and palaces to those who are huddled around radios in the forgotten corners of our world—our stories are singular, but our destiny is shared, and a new dawn of American leadership is at hand. To those—to those who would tear this world down—we will defeat you. To those who seek peace and security—we support you. And to all those who have wondered if America's beacon still burns as bright—tonight we proved once more that the true strength of our nation comes not from the might of our arms or the scale of our wealth, but from the enduring power of our ideals: democracy, liberty, opportunity, and unyielding hope.

That's the true genius of America—that America can change. Our union can be perfected. What we've already achieved gives us hope for what we can and must achieve tomorrow.

This election had many firsts and many stories that will be told for generations. But one that's on my mind tonight's about a woman who cast her ballot in Atlanta. She's a lot like the millions of others who stood in line to make their voice heard in this election except for one thing—Ann Nixon Cooper is 106 years old.

She was born just a generation past slavery; a time when there were no cars on the road or planes in the sky; when someone like her couldn't vote for two reasons—because she was a woman and because of the color of her skin.

And tonight, I think about all that she's seen throughout her century in America—the heartache and the hope; the struggle and the progress; the times we were told that we can't, and the people who pressed on with that American creed: Yes we can.

At a time when women's voices were silenced and their hopes dismissed, she lived to see them stand up and speak out and reach for the ballot. Yes we can.

When there was despair in the dust bowl and depression across the land, she saw a nation conquer fear itself with a New Deal, new jobs, a new sense of common purpose. Yes we can.

When the bombs fell on our harbor and tyranny threatened the world, she was there to witness a generation rise to greatness and a democracy was saved. Yes we can.

She was there for the buses in Montgomery, the hoses in Birmingham, a bridge in Selma, and a preacher from Atlanta who told a people that "We Shall Overcome." Yes we can.

A man touched down on the moon, a wall came down in Berlin, a world was connected by our own science and imagination. And this year, in this election, she touched her finger to a screen, and cast her vote, because after 106 years in America, through the best of times and the darkest of hours, she knows how America can change. Yes we can.

America, we have come so far. We have seen so much. But there is so much more to do. So tonight, let us ask ourselves— if our children should live to see the next century; if my daughters should be so lucky to live as long as Ann Nixon Cooper, what change will they see? What progress will we have made?

This is our chance to answer that call. This is our moment. This is our time—to put our people back to work and open doors of opportunity for our kids; to restore prosperity and promote the cause of peace; to reclaim the American Dream and reaffirm that fundamental truth—that out of many, we are one; that while we breathe, we hope; and where we are met with cynicism, and doubts, and those who tell us that we can't, we will respond with that timeless creed that sums up the spirit of a people: Yes we can.

Thank you, God bless you, and may God Bless the United States of America.

INAUGURAL ADDRESS

January 20, 2009 | *Washington, D.C.*

M Y FELLOW CITIZENS:
      I stand here today humbled by the task before us,
grateful for the trust you have bestowed, mindful of the
sacrifices borne by our ancestors. I thank President Bush
for his service to our nation, as well as the generosity and
cooperation he has shown throughout this transition.

Forty-four Americans have now taken the presidential
oath. The words have been spoken during rising tides of
prosperity and the still waters of peace. Yet, every so often
the oath is taken amidst gathering clouds and raging storms.
At these moments, America has carried on not simply
because of the skill or vision of those in high office, but
because We the People have remained faithful to the ideals
of our forebears, and true to our founding documents.

So it has been. So it must be with this generation of
Americans.

That we are in the midst of crisis is now well understood. Our nation is at war against a far-reaching network

of violence and hatred. Our economy is badly weakened, a consequence of greed and irresponsibility on the part of some but also our collective failure to make hard choices and prepare the nation for a new age. Homes have been lost, jobs shed, businesses shuttered. Our health care is too costly, our schools fail too many, and each day brings further evidence that the ways we use energy strengthen our adversaries and threaten our planet.

These are the indicators of crisis, subject to data and statistics. Less measurable, but no less profound, is a sapping of confidence across our land; a nagging fear that America's decline is inevitable, that the next generation must lower its sights.

Today I say to you that the challenges we face are real, they are serious and they are many. They will not be met easily or in a short span of time. But know this America: They will be met.

On this day, we gather because we have chosen hope over fear, unity of purpose over conflict and discord.

On this day, we come to proclaim an end to the petty grievances and false promises, the recriminations and worn-out dogmas that for far too long have strangled our politics.

We remain a young nation, but in the words of Scripture, the time has come to set aside childish things. The time has come to reaffirm our enduring spirit; to choose our better history; to carry forward that precious gift, that noble idea, passed on from generation to generation: the God-given promise that all are equal, all are free, and all deserve a chance to pursue their full measure of happiness.

In reaffirming the greatness of our nation, we understand that greatness is never a given. It must be earned. Our journey has never been one of shortcuts or settling for less. It has not been the path for the faint-hearted, for those who prefer leisure over work, or seek only the pleasures of riches and fame. Rather, it has been the risk-takers, the doers, the makers of things—some celebrated, but more often men and women obscure in their labor—who have carried us up the long, rugged path towards prosperity and freedom.

For us, they packed up their few worldly possessions and traveled across oceans in search of a new life.

For us, they toiled in sweatshops and settled the West, endured the lash of the whip and plowed the hard earth.

For us, they fought and died in places like Concord and Gettysburg; Normandy and Khe Sanh.

Time and again these men and women struggled and sacrificed and worked till their hands were raw so that we might live a better life. They saw America as bigger than the sum of our individual ambitions; greater than all the differences of birth or wealth or faction.

This is the journey we continue today. We remain the most prosperous, powerful nation on Earth. Our workers are no less productive than when this crisis began. Our minds are no less inventive, our goods and services no less needed than they were last week or last month or last year. Our capacity remains undiminished. But our time of standing pat, of protecting narrow interests and putting off unpleasant decisions—that time has surely passed. Starting today, we must pick ourselves up, dust ourselves off, and begin again the work of remaking America.

For everywhere we look, there is work to be done. The state of our economy calls for action, bold and swift. And we will act not only to create new jobs but to lay a new foundation for growth. We will build the roads and bridges, the electric grids and digital lines that feed our commerce and bind us together. We will restore science to its rightful place and wield technology's wonders to raise health care's quality and lower its costs. We will harness the sun and the winds and the soil to fuel our cars and run our factories. And we will transform our schools and colleges and universities to meet the demands of a new age. All this we can do. All this we will do.

Now, there are some who question the scale of our ambitions, who suggest that our system cannot tolerate too many big plans. Their memories are short, for they have forgotten what this country has already done, what free men and women can achieve when imagination is joined to common purpose and necessity to courage.

What the cynics fail to understand is that the ground has shifted beneath them, that the stale political arguments that have consumed us for so long no longer apply. The question we ask today is not whether our government is too big or too small, but whether it works, whether it helps families find jobs at a decent wage, care they can afford, a retirement that is dignified. Where the answer is yes, we intend to move forward. Where the answer is no, programs will end. And those of us who manage the public's dollars will be held to account, to spend wisely, reform bad habits, and do our business in the light of day, because only then can we restore the vital trust between a people and their government.

Nor is the question before us whether the market is a force for good or ill. Its power to generate wealth and expand freedom is unmatched. But this crisis has reminded us that without a watchful eye, the market can spin out of control. The nation cannot prosper long when it favors only the prosperous. The success of our economy has always depended not just on the size of our gross domestic product, but on the reach of our prosperity; on the ability to extend opportunity to every willing heart—not out of charity, but because it is the surest route to our common good.

As for our common defense, we reject as false the choice between our safety and our ideals. Our founding fathers, faced with perils that we can scarcely imagine, drafted a charter to assure the rule of law and the rights of man, a charter expanded by the blood of generations. Those ideals still light the world, and we will not give them up for expedience's sake. And so, to all other peoples and governments who are watching today, from the grandest capitals to the small village where my father was born: know that America is a friend of each nation and every man, woman and child who seeks a future of peace and dignity, and we are ready to lead once more.

Recall that earlier generations faced down fascism and communism not just with missiles and tanks, but with the sturdy alliances and enduring convictions. They understood that our power alone cannot protect us, nor does it entitle us to do as we please. Instead, they knew that our power grows through its prudent use. Our security emanates from the justness of our cause; the force of our example; the tempering qualities of humility and restraint.

We are the keepers of this legacy. Guided by these principles once more, we can meet those new threats that demand even greater effort, even greater cooperation and understanding between nations. We'll begin to responsibly leave Iraq to its people and forge a hard-earned peace in Afghanistan. With old friends and former foes, we'll work tirelessly to lessen the nuclear threat and roll back the specter of a warming planet. We will not apologize for our way of life nor will we waver in its defense. And for those who seek to advance their aims by inducing terror and slaughtering innocents, we say to you now, "Our spirit is stronger and cannot be broken. You cannot outlast us, and we will defeat you."

For we know that our patchwork heritage is a strength, not a weakness. We are a nation of Christians and Muslims, Jews and Hindus, and nonbelievers. We are shaped by every language and culture, drawn from every end of this Earth. And because we have tasted the bitter swill of civil war and segregation and emerged from that dark chapter stronger and more united, we cannot help but believe that the old hatreds shall someday pass; that the lines of tribe shall soon dissolve; that as the world grows smaller, our common humanity shall reveal itself; and that America must play its role in ushering in a new era of peace.

To the Muslim world, we seek a new way forward, based on mutual interest and mutual respect. To those leaders around the globe who seek to sow conflict or blame their society's ills on the West, know that your people will judge you on what you can build, not what you destroy. To those who cling to power through corruption and deceit and the silencing of dissent, know that you are on the wrong side of history, but that we will extend a hand if you are willing to unclench your fist.

To the people of poor nations, we pledge to work alongside you to make your farms flourish and let clean waters flow; to nourish starved bodies and feed hungry minds. And to those nations like ours that enjoy relative plenty, we say we can no longer afford indifference to the suffering outside our borders, nor can we consume the world's resources without regard to effect. For the world has changed, and we must change with it.

As we consider the road that unfolds before us, we remember with humble gratitude those brave Americans who, at this very hour, patrol far-off deserts and distant mountains. They have something to tell us, just as the fallen heroes who lie in Arlington whisper through the ages. We honor them not only because they are guardians of our liberty, but because they embody the spirit of service: a willingness to find meaning in something greater than themselves. And yet, at this moment, a moment that will define a generation, it is precisely this spirit that must inhabit us all.

For as much as government can do and must do, it is ultimately the faith and determination of the American people upon which this nation relies. It is the kindness to take in a stranger when the levees break; the selflessness of workers who would rather cut their hours than see a friend lose their job which sees us through our darkest hours. It is the firefighter's courage to storm a stairway filled with smoke, but also a parent's willingness to nurture a child, that finally decides our fate.

Our challenges may be new, the instruments with which we meet them may be new, but those values upon which our success depends, honesty and hard work, courage and fair play, tolerance and curiosity, loyalty and patriotism— these things are old. These things are true. They have been the quiet force of progress throughout our history. What is demanded then is a return to these truths. What is required of us now is a new era of responsibility—a recognition, on the part of every American, that we have duties to ourselves, our nation and the world, duties that we do not grudgingly accept but rather seize gladly, firm in the knowledge that there is nothing so satisfying to the spirit, so defining of our character than giving our all to a difficult task.

This is the price and the promise of citizenship.

This is the source of our confidence: the knowledge that God calls on us to shape an uncertain destiny.

This is the meaning of our liberty and our creed, why men and women and children of every race and every faith can join in celebration across this magnificent mall. And why a man whose father less than 60 years ago might not have been served at a local restaurant can now stand before you to take a most sacred oath.

So let us mark this day in remembrance of who we are and how far we have traveled. In the year of America's birth, in the coldest of months, a small band of patriots huddled by dying campfires on the shores of an icy river. The capital was abandoned. The enemy was advancing. The snow was stained with blood. At a moment when the outcome of our revolution was most in doubt, the father of our nation ordered these words be read to the people:

"Let it be told to the future world that in the depth of winter, when nothing but hope and virtue could survive, that the city and the country, alarmed at one common danger, came forth to meet it."

America, in the face of our common dangers, in this winter of our hardship, let us remember these timeless words; with hope and virtue, let us brave once more the icy currents, and endure what storms may come; let it be said by our children's children that when we were tested we refused to let this journey end, that we did not turn back nor did we falter; and with eyes fixed on the horizon and God's grace upon us, we carried forth that great gift of freedom and delivered it safely to future generations.

Thank you. God bless you.

And God bless the United States of America.

Acknowledgments

Special thanks to Andrei Cherny and Kenneth Baer for countless hours of work and support.

Thanks to "Team Book" at Obama for America: Jim Messina, Heather Higginbottom, Karen Dunn, Madhuri Kommareddi, Jon Favreau, Anita Dunn, Dan Pfeiffer, Larry Grisolano, Brian Levine, Terry Walsh, Peter Giangreco, Shauna Daly, and Bob Bauer and his team at Perkins Coie. And to the best book lawyer in the business, Bob Barnett.

Rachel "Yes We Can" Klayman is a superb editor and a true professional. This book could not and would not have been published without her. Publisher Jenny Frost's leadership allowed this book to be published and in the stores in record time. Obama for America thanks them both. We also thank the other members of the Crown team: Lucinda Bartley, Tina Constable, Linda Kaplan, Linnea Knollmueller, Philip Patrick, Dan Rembert, Annsley Rosner, and Katie Wainwright. We are especially grateful for the skill and dedication shown by Amy Boorstein, Mary Choteborsky, Barbara Sturman, and the entire production editorial department at Crown.

And to every American who wants change we can believe in.

Barack Obama was born in Honolulu in 1961. In his early twenties he found his vocation working among poor communities on the south side of Chicago. Later he went to law school at Harvard University, where he became the first black president of the *Harvard Law Review*. In 1995 he published his memoir *Dreams from My Father*, which became a bestseller soon after it was reissued in 2004. After returning to Chicago, he was elected to the Illinois State Senate in 1996.

Barack Obama delivered the keynote address at the 2004 Democratic National Convention, and later that year he was elected to the US Senate. His second book, *The Audacity of Hope*, was published in 2006 and became an immediate bestseller. In November 2008 Senator Obama was elected the 44th President of the United States of America. He is married to Michelle, with whom he has two daughters, Sasha and Malia.